A SKETCH
OF THE
GEOGRAPHY AND GEOLOGY
OF THE
HIMALAYA MOUNTAINS AND TIBET

BY

COLONEL S. G. BURRARD, R.E., F.R.S.,
SUPERINTENDENT, TRIGONOMETRICAL SURVEYS,

AND

H. H. HAYDEN, B.A., F.G.S., (later Sir Henry Hayden, Kt., C.S.I., C.I.E)
SUPERINTENDENT, GEOLOGICAL SURVEY OF INDIA,

REVISED BY

COLONEL SIR SIDNEY BURRARD, K.C.S.I., F.R.S.,

AND

A. M. HERON, D. Sc., F.G.S., F.R.G.S., F.R.S.E.,
SUPERINTENDENT, GEOLOGICAL SURVEY OF INDIA.

PART I
THE HIGH PEAKS OF ASIA

Published by order of the Government of India.

DELHI: MANAGER OF PUBLICATIONS
1933

Sold at the Office of the Geodetic Branch, Survey of India, Dehra Dun.

Government of India Publications are obtainable from the Manager of Publications, Civil Lines, Delhi, and from the following Agents:—

EUROPE.

OFFICE OF THE HIGH COMMISSIONER FOR INDIA, India House, Aldwych, LONDON, W.C. 2

And at all Booksellers.

INDIA AND CEYLON : Provincial Book Depôts.

MADRAS :—Superintendent, Government Press, Mount Road, Madras.
BOMBAY :—Superintendent, Government Printing and Stationery, Queen's Road, Bombay.
SIND :—Library attached to the Office of the Commissioner in Sind, Karachi.
BENGAL :—Bengal Secretariat Book Depôt, Writers' Buildings, Room No. 1, Ground Floor, Calcutta.
UNITED PROVINCES OF AGRA AND OUDH :—Superintendent of Government Press, United Provinces of Agra and Oudh, Allahabad.
PUNJAB :—Superintendent, Government Printing, Punjab, Lahore.
BURMA :—Superintendent, Government Printing, Burma, Rangoon.
CENTRAL PROVINCES AND BERAR :—Superintendent, Government Printing, Central Provinces, Nagpur.
ASSAM :—Superintendent, Assam Secretariat Press, Shillong.
BIHAR AND ORISSA :—Superintendent, Government Printing, Bihar and Orissa, P. O. Gulzarbagh, Patna.
NORTH-WEST FRONTIER PROVINCE :—Manager, Government Printing and Stationery, Peshawar.

Thacker, Spink & Co., Ltd., Calcutta and Simla.
W. Newman & Co., Ltd., Calcutta.
S. K. Lahiri & Co., Calcutta.
The Indian School Supply Depôt, 309, Bow Bazar Street, Calcutta.
Butterworth & Co. (India), Ltd., Calcutta.
M. C. Sarcar & Sons, 15, College Square, Calcutta.
Standard Literature Company, Limited, Calcutta.
Association Press, Calcutta.
Chukervertty, Chatterjee & Co., Ltd., 13, College Square, Calcutta.
The Book Company, Calcutta.
James Murray & Co., 12, Government Place, Calcutta. (For Meteorological Publications only).
Ray Chaudhury & Co., 68-5, Ashutosh Mukherji Road, Calcutta.
Scientific Publishing Co., 9, Taltola Lane, Calcutta.
Chatterjee & Co., 3-1, Bacharam Chatterjee Lane, Calcutta.
Standard Law Book Society, 5, Hastings Street, Calcutta.
The Hindu Library, 3, Nandalal Mullick Lane, Calcutta.
Kamala Book Depôt, Ltd., 15, College Square, Calcutta.
The Pioneer Book Supply Co., 20, Shibnarain Das Lane, Calcutta.
P. C. Sarkar & Co., 2, Shama Charan De Street, Calcutta.
Bengal Flying Club, Dum Dum Cantt.
Kali Charan & Co., Municipal Market, Calcutta.
N. M. Roy Chowdhury & Co., 11, College Sqr., Calcutta.
Grantha Mandir, Cuttack.
B. C. Basak, Esq., Proprietor, Albert Library, Dacca.
Higginbothams, Madras.
Rochouse and Sons, Madras.
G. A. Natesan & Co., Publishers, George Town, Madras.
P. Varadachary & Co., Madras.
City Book Co., Madras.
Law Publishing Co., Mylapore, Madras.
The Booklover's Resort, Taikad, Trivandrum, South India.
E. M. Gopalakrishna Kone, Pudumandapam, Madura.
Central Book Depôt, Madura.
Vijapur & Co., Vizagapatam.
Thacker & Co., Ltd., Bombay.
D. B. Taraporevala, Sons & Co., Bombay.
Ram Chandra Govind & Sons, Kalbadevi Road, Bombay.
N. M. Tripathi & Co., Booksellers, Princess Street, Kalbadevi Road, Bombay.
New and Secondhand Bookshop, Kalbadevi Road, Bombay.
J. M. Pandia & Co., Bombay.
A. H. Wheeler & Co., Allahabad, Calcutta and Bombay.
Bombay Book Depôt, Girgaon, Bombay.
Bennett, Coleman & Co., Ltd., The Times of India Press, Bombay.
The Popular Book Depôt, Bombay.
Lawrence and Mayo, Ltd., Bombay.
The Manager, Oriental Book Supplying Agency, 15, Shukrawar, Poona City.
Rama Krishna Bros., Opposite Bishrambag, Poona City.
S. P. Bookstall, 21, Budhwar, Poona.
The International Book Service, Poona 4.
Mangaldas & Sons, Booksellers and Publishers, Bhaga Talao, Surat.
The Standard Book and Stationery Co., 32-33, Arbab Road, Peshawar.
The Students Own Book Depôt, Dharwar.
Shri Shankar Karnataka Pustaka Bhandara Malamuddi, Dharwar.
The English Book Depôt, Ferozepore.
Frontier Book & Stationery Co., Rawalpindi.
*Hossenbhoy Karimji and Sons, Karachi.
The English Bookstall, Karachi.
Rose & Co., Karachi.
Kean & Co., Karachi.
Ram Chander & Sons, Ambala, Kasauli.
The Standard Bookstall, Quetta and Lahore.
U. P. Malhotra & Co., Quetta.
J. Ray & Sons, 43, K. & L., Edwardes Road, Rawalpindi, Murree and Lahore.
The Standard Book Depôt, Lahore, Nainital, Mussoorie, Dalhousie, Ambala Cantonment and Delhi.
The North India Christian Tract and Book Society, 18, Clive Road, Allahabad.
Ram Narain Lal, Katra, Allahabad.
"The Leader", Allahabad.
The Indian Army Book Depôt, Dayalbagh, Agra.
The English Book Depôt, Taj Road, Agra.
Gaya Prasad & Sons, Agra.
Narain & Co., Meston Road, Cawnpore.
The Indian Army Book Depôt, Jullundur City—Daryaganj, Delhi.
Manager, Newal Kishore Press, Lucknow.
The Upper India Publishing House, Ltd., Literature Palace, Ammuddaula Park, Lucknow.
Rai Sahib M. Gulab Singh & Sons, Mufid-i-Am Press, Lahore and Allahabad.
Rama Krishna & Sons, Booksellers, Anarkali, Lahore.
Students Popular Depôt, Anarkali, Lahore.
The Proprietor, Punjab Sanskrit Book Depôt, Saidmitha Street, Lahore.
The Insurance Publicity Co., Ltd., Lahore.
The Punjab Religious Book Society, Lahore.
The Commercial Book Co., Lahore.
The University Book Agency, Kachari Road, Lahore.
Manager of the Imperial Book Depôt, 63, Chandni Chowk Street, Delhi.
J. M. Jaina & Bros., Delhi.
Fono Book Agency, New Delhi and Simla.
Oxford Book and Stationery Company, Delhi, Lahore, Simla, Meerut and Calcutta.
Mohanlal Dossabhai Shah, Rajkot.
Supdt., American Baptist Mission Press, Rangoon.
Burma Book Club, Ltd., Rangoon.
S. C. Talukdar, Proprietor, Students & Co., Cooch Behar.
The Manager, The Indian Book Shop, Benares City.
Nandkishore & Bros., Chowk, Benares City.
The Srivilliputtur Co-operative Trading Union, Ltd., Srivilliputtur (S. I. R.)
Raghunath Prasad & Sons, Patna City.
The Students' Emporium, Patna.
K. L. Mathur & Bros., Guzri, Patna City.
Kamala Book Stores, Bankipore, Patna.
G. Banerjee and Bros., Ranchi.
M. C. Kothari, Raipura Road, Baroda.
R. Parikh & Co., Baroda.
The Hyderabad Book Depôt, Chaderghat, Hyderabad (Deccan).
S. Krishnaswamy & Co., Teppakulam P. O., Trichinopoly Fort.
Standard Book and Map Agency, Book Sellers and Publishers, Ballygunge.
Karnataka Publishing House, Bangalore City.
Bheema Sons, Fort, Bangalore City.
Superintendent, Bangalore Press, Lake View, Mysore Road, Bangalore City.

AGENT IN PALESTINE :—Steimatzky, Jerusalem.
* Agents for publications on aviation only.

PREFACE TO THE FIRST (1907) EDITION

IN 1807 a Survey detachment was deputed by the Surveyor General of Bengal to explore the source of the Ganges: this was the first expedition to the Himalaya undertaken for purely geographical purposes. A hundred years have now elapsed, during which geographical and geological information has been steadily accumulating, and we have at length reached a stage where there is danger of losing our way in a maze of unclassified detail: it is therefore desirable to review our present position, to co-ordinate our varied observations and to see how far we have progressed and what directions appear favourable for future lines of advance.

The present paper originated in a proposal submitted by the Survey of India to the Board of Scientific Advice at the meeting of the latter in May 1906. The proposal was as follows:—" The number of travellers in the Himālaya and Tibet " is increasing, and a wider interest is being evinced by the public in the geography " of these regions. It is therefore proposed to compile a paper summarising the " geographical position at the present time ".

Subject to the modification that the scope of the paper should be geological as well as geographical, this proposal has received the sanction of the Government of India and the work has been entrusted to us to carry out. On the understanding that the paper is intended primarily for the use of the public, we have endeavoured to avoid purely technical details and to present our results in a popular manner.

Our subject has fallen naturally into four parts, as follows:—

PART I.—The high peaks of Asia.
PART II.—The principal mountain ranges of Asia.
PART III.—The rivers of the Himālaya and Tibet.
PART IV.—The geology of the Himālaya.

Though the four parts are essentially interdependent, each has been made as far as possible complete in itself and will be published separately. The first three parts are mainly geographical, the fourth part is wholly geological: the parts are subdivided into sections, and against each section in the table of contents is given the name of the author responsible for it.

The endeavour to render each part complete must be our apology for having repeated ourselves in more places than one: the relations, for instance, of a range to a river have been discussed in Part II, when the range was being described, and have been mentioned again in Part III under the account of the river.

As the mountains of Asia become more accurately surveyed, errors will doubtless be found in what we have written and drawn: it is not possible yet to arrive at correct generalisations and we have to be content with first approximations to truth.

PREFACE TO THE FIRST (1907) EDITION—*contd.*

Maps, too large for insertion in such a volume as this, are required for a study of the Himālayan mountains: the titles of maps illustrating the text are given in footnotes and are procurable from the Map Issue Office of the Survey of India in Calcutta. Constable's hand-atlas of India will be found useful.

We are much indebted to Babus Shiv Nath Saha and Ishan Chandra Dev, B.A., for the care with which they have checked our figures and names, and to Mr. J. H. Nichol for the trouble he has taken to ensure the correctness of the charts. Mr. Eccles and Major Lenox Conyngham have been kind enough to examine all proofs, and to give us the benefit of their advice and suggestions. Mr. Eccles has also supervised the drawing and printing of the charts, and we have profited greatly by the interest he has shown in them.

S. G. BURRARD.

H. H. HAYDEN.

March 1907.

PREFACE TO THE SECOND (1932) EDITION

THIS book on the Himālaya Mountains and Tibet was originally compiled as a centenary review of the geographical and geological knowledge which had been gained during 1807-1907. The book has proved invaluable as a work of reference for surveyors and explorers, and there has been a steady public demand for it both in India and Europe.

As the original edition printed in 1907 has become exhausted it has been deemed very desirable to issue a second edition and to have this brought up to date. Of the two authors who jointly prepared the original book, Sir Henry Hayden was killed on the Alps by a fall of rock in 1923, and Sir Sidney Burrard retired from the service in 1919. Sir Sidney Burrard was asked if he would be willing to undertake the revision of the geographical portions, and this he has most kindly undertaken in collaboration with the Geodetic Branch office. The great advantage of having this important work re-written as regards its geographical portions by an original author of the unique standing of Sir Sidney Burrard is very cordially recognised.

The task of revising Sir Henry Hayden's geological contributions and of bringing them up to date has been entrusted to Dr. A. M. Heron, who requests that acknowledgment may be made of the help given by Dr. G. de P. Cotter in questions of geological correlation, and by Messrs. D. N. Wadia, W. D. West and J. B. Auden in the compilation of the geological maps of the Himālaya that accompany this work.

R. H. THOMAS, *Brigadier,*
Surveyor General of India.

L. L. FERMOR,
Offg. Director, Geological Survey of India.

March 1932.

CONTENTS OF PART I.

	PAGE.
Preface to 1907 (first) Edition	i
Preface to 1932 (second) Edition	iii
Chapter 1. The principal peaks and their altitudes. (*S. G. Burrard*)	1
Chapter 2. The evolution of geographical names in the Himālaya. (*S. G. Burrard*)	7
Chapter 3. Geographical names that have given rise to controversy. (*S. G. Burrard*)	13
Chapter 4. Notes on certain important mountain names. (*S. G. Burrard*)	40
Chapter 5. On the errors of the adopted values of height. (*S. G. Burrard*)	53
Chapter 6. The geology of the great peaks. (*H. H. Hayden*, revised by *A. M. Heron*)	63
Appendix 1. A synopsis of the Linguistic Survey of India. (*S. G. Burrard*)	67

CHARTS AND PLATES.

Chart to illustrate the trends of the principal mountain ranges of the Himālayan and Tibetan systems.	Frontispiece.
Pictures by Colonel G. Strahan, R.E.	facing p. 6
Nojli Tower	facing p. 53
Chart I. Peaks of the first magnitude	
Chart II. Peaks of the second and first magnitudes	
Chart III. Peaks of the third and higher magnitudes	
Chart IV. Peaks of the fourth and higher magnitudes	at the end.
Chart V. Peaks of the fifth and higher magnitudes	
Chart VI. Panoramas of the Himālaya in Nepāl and Sikkim	
Chart VII. Panorama of the Himālaya in Kumaun	
Chart VIII. Panorama of the Himālaya between the Ganges and Sutlej	

INDEX

See Part III.

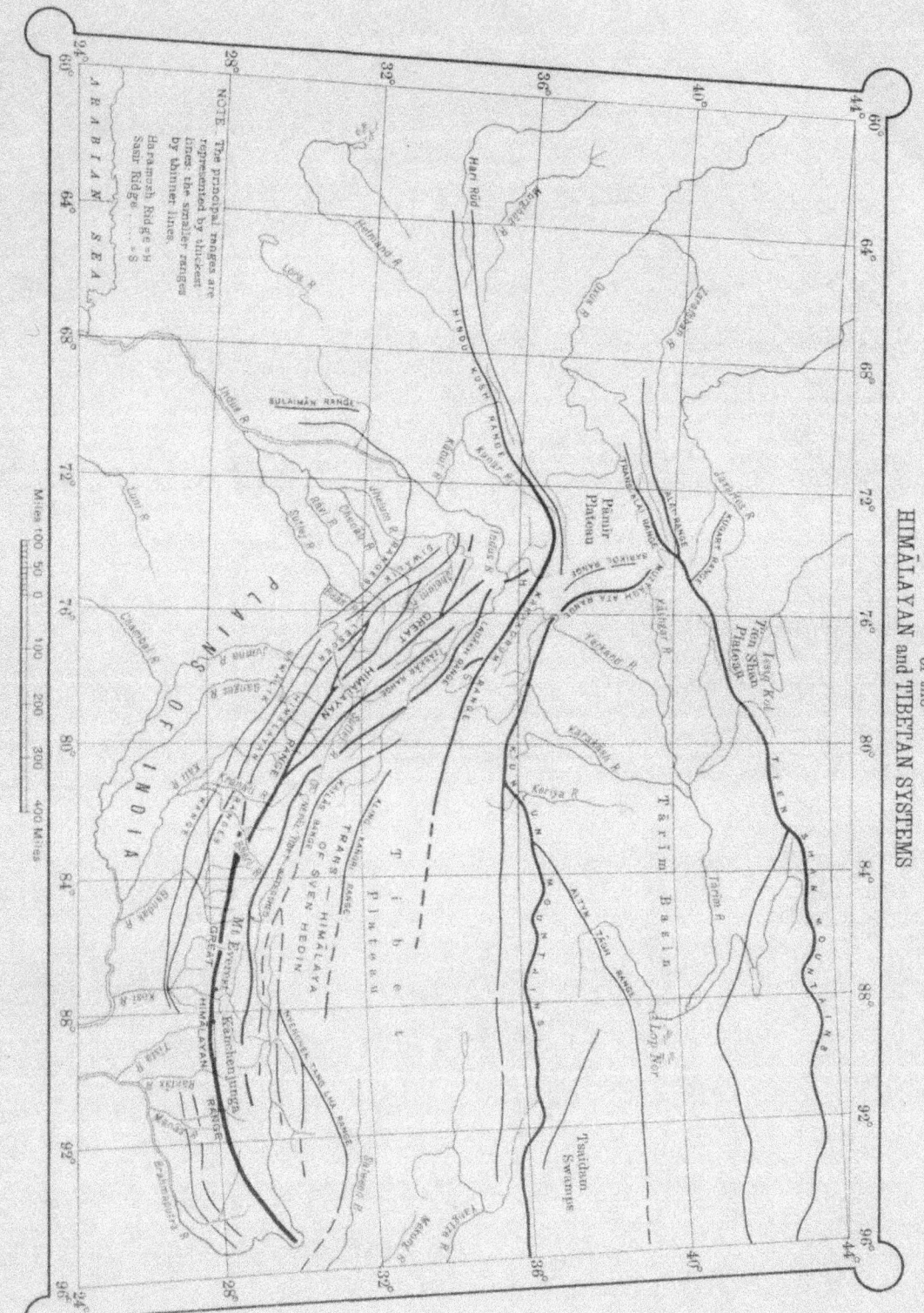

THE HIGH PEAKS OF ASIA.

CHAPTER 1.

THE PRINCIPAL PEAKS AND THEIR ALTITUDES.

IN the earlier stages of geographical investigation the most important features of a mountain mass are the high peaks. They may be, it is true, but slight prominences of lofty ranges and they may possess perhaps no geological significance; but they are conspicuous and definite points; they are the only mountain features that can be observed with accuracy from a distance; and the determination of their positions and heights is the first step of the ladder of geographical knowledge. When this step has been taken, further progress becomes possible; the peaks can be made the basis of subsequent surveys; the courses of rivers and the positions of lakes can be laid down with regard to them; the trends and forms and magnitudes of the ranges can be inferred from the distribution of the peaks.

In the following Tables I to V all the peaks of Asia that have been found to exceed 24,000 feet in height are catalogued in order of magnitude: their geographical positions are shown in the five corresponding charts, numbered also I to V.

TABLE I.—Peaks of the first magnitude, exceeding 28,000 feet in height.

Reference Number of Peak.	Name or Symbol.	Peak and Sheet Numbers.	Number of stations from which the height was observed.	System.	Height.	Latitude.	Longitude.
1	2	3	4	5	6	7	8
1	Mount Everest	37/72 I	6	Nepāl Himālaya	*feet* 29,002	° ′ ″ 27 59 16	° ′ ″ 86 55 40
2	K²	13/52 A	9	Karakorum	28,250	35 52 55	76 30 51
3	Kānchenjunga	10¹/78 A	9	Nepāl Himālaya	28,146	27 42 09	88 09 00

TABLE II.—Peaks of the second magnitude, between 27,000 and 28,000 feet in height.

Reference Number of Peak.	Name or Symbol.	Peak and Sheet Numbers.	Number of stations from which the height was observed.	System.	Height.	Latitude.	Longitude.
1	2	3	4	5	6	7	8
4	E¹	Sheet 72 I	..	Nepāl Himālaya	*feet* 27,890	° ′ ″ 27 57 43	° ′ ″ 86 56 10
5	Kānchenjunga II	10²/78 A	7	Nepāl Himālaya	27,803	27 41 30	88 09 24
6	Makālu	2/72 M	6	Nepāl Himālaya	27,790	27 53 23	87 05 29

TABLE III.—Peaks of the third magnitude, between 26,000 and 27,000 feet in height.

Reference Number of Peak.	Name or Symbol.	Peak and Sheet Numbers.	Number of stations from which the height was observed.	System.	Height.	Latitude.	Longitude.
1	2	3	4	5	6	7	8
					feet	° ′ ″	° ′ ″
7	Dhaulāgiri	9/62 P	7	Nepāl Himālaya	26,795	28 41 48	83 29 42
8	Cho Oyu	5/71 L	5	Nepāl Himālaya	26,750	28 05 32	86 39 51
9	Kutang I	14/71 D	3	Nepāl Himālaya	26,658	28 33 00	84 33 43
10	Nanga Parbat I	48/43 I	8	Punjab Himālaya	26,629	35 14 21	74 35 24
11	Annapurna I	Sheet 62 P	8	Nepāl Himālaya	26,492	28 35 44	83 49 19
12	Gasherbrum I	23/52 A	4	Karakorum	26,470	35 43 30	76 41 48
13	Broad Peak	16/52 A	..	Karakorum	26,400	35 48 35	76 34 23
14	Gasherbrum II	21/52 A	2	Karakorum	26,360	35 45 31	76 39 15
15	Gosainthān	46/71 H	2	Nepāl Himālaya	26,291	28 21 07	85 46 55
16	Gasherbrum IV	19/52 A	2	Karakorum	26,180	35 45 38	76 37 02
17	Gasherbrum III	20/52 A	2	Karakorum	26,090	35 45 36	76 38 33
18	Annapurna II	3/71 D	5	Nepāl Himālaya	26,041	28 32 05	84 07 26

TABLE IV.—Peaks of the fourth magnitude, between 25,000 and 26,000 feet in height.

Reference Number of Peak.	Name or Symbol.	Peak and Sheet Numbers.	Number of stations from which the height was observed.	System.	Height.	Latitude.	Longitude.
1	2	3	4	5	6	7	8
					feet	° ′ ″	° ′ ″
19	Gyachung Kang	3/71 L	1	Nepāl Himālaya	25,990	28 05 52	86 44 41
20	Disto Ghil	20/42 P	2	Karakorum	25,868	36 19 35	75 11 20
21	Himalchuli	19/71 D	4	Nepāl Himālaya	25,801	28 26 03	84 38 34
22	Kangbachen	9/78 A	4	Nepāl Himālaya	25,782	27 42 59	88 06 47
23	Ngojamba Kang	2/71 L	4	Nepāl Himālaya	25,730	28 06 24	86 41 15
24	Kutang II	16/71 D	2	Nepāl Himālaya	25,705	28 30 12	84 34 07
25	E³	Sheet 72 I	..	Nepāl Himālaya	25,700	27 57 53	86 53 23
26	Masherbrum East	7/52 A	7	Karakorum	25,660	35 38 36	76 18 31
27	Nanda Devi	115/53 N	9	Kumaun Himālaya	25,645	30 22 32	79 58 22
28	Chomo Lonzo	1/72 M	2	Nepāl Himālaya	25,640	27 55 47	87 06 44
29	Masherbrum West	8/52 A	3	Karakorum	25,610	35 38 29	76 18 23
30	Nanga Parbat II	47/43 I	2	Punjab Himālaya	25,572	35 15 22	74 35 14
31	Rakaposhi	27/42 L	3	Haramosh Ridge	25,550	36 08 39	74 29 22
32	Hunza-Kunji I	32/42 L	3	Karakorum	25,540	36 30 39	74 31 26
33	Kunjut No. 1	12/42 P	2	Karakorum	25,460	36 12 21	75 25 03
34	Kāmet	49/53 N	6	Zāskār Range	25,447	30 55 13	79 35 37
35	Namcha Barwa	5/82 O	..	Assam Himālaya	25,445	29 37 51	95 03 31
36	XLIII	5/62 P	5	Nepāl Himālaya	25,429	28 45 45	83 23 25
37	Sherpigang I	36/52 A	4	Karakorum	25,400	35 24 01	76 56 55
38	Gurla Mandhāta	7/62 F	2	Nepāl Tibet Watershed.	25,355	30 26 18	81 17 57
39	Jano	13/78 A	9	Nepāl Himālaya	25,294	27 40 56	88 02 47
40	Hunza-Kunji II	31/42 L	1	Karakorum	25,294	36 31 54	74 30 01
41	Sherpigang II	35/52 A	4	Karakorum	25,280	35 24 24	76 50 30
42	K²²	29/52 F	2	Sasir Ridge	25,280	34 52 00	77 45 13
43	XLIV	6/62 P	3	Nepāl Himālaya	25,271	28 45 13	83 22 46
44	Tirich Mīr I	7/37 P	2	Hindu Kush	25,263	36 15 21	71 50 32
45	B³⁹⁴	44/71 H	2	Nepāl Himālaya	25,134	28 21 17	85 48 45
46	Makālu II	Sheet 72 M	..	Nepāl Himālaya	25,120	27 54 58	87 04 54
47	Chogolisa	25/52 A	4	Karakorum	25,110	35 36 44	76 34 23
48	Satellite of Gosainthān	7/62 P	7	Nepāl Himālaya	25,064	28 44 07	83 18 53
49	Kungur *	4/42 N	2	Muztāgh Ata	25,146	38 39 23	75 13 05

* Sir Aurel Stein prefers the spelling Kongur.

Correction to "A sketch of the Geography and Geology of the Himalaya Mountains and Tibet (1933)".

Part I, page 2, Table IV, column 2, second line from bottom:
For "Satellite of Gosainthān" *substitute* "Satellite of Dhaulāgiri".
No. 1, dated 7-6-35.

G.B.—P.O.—J.S. 392—7-6-35—1,050.

TABLE V.—Peaks of the fifth magnitude, between 24,000 and 25,000 feet in height.

Reference Number of Peak.	Name or Symbol.	Peak and Sheet Numbers.	Number of stations from which the height was observed.	System.	Height.	Latitude.	Longitude.
1	2	3	4	5	6	7	8
					feet	° ′ ″	° ′ ″
50	Boiohaghŭrduânasîr	33/42 L	8	Karakorum	24,970	36 26 30	74 40 52
51	XLV	8/62 P	5	Nepâl Himâlaya	24,885	28 44 03	83 21 51
52	Kula Kangri I	19/77 L	2	Assam Himâlaya	24,784	28 14 02	90 37 09
53	XXXVI	18/62 P	4	Nepâl Himâlaya	24,750	28 35 03	83 59 31
54	Kula Kangri II	13/77 L	4	Assam Himâlaya	24,740	28 02 49	90 27 30
55	E²	Sheet 71 L	..	Nepâl Himâlaya	24,730	28 01 27	86 54 47
56	Kula Kangri III	12/77 L	1	Assam Himâlaya	24,710	28 03 13	90 27 28
57	Mamostong	12/52 E	1	Karakorum	24,690	35 08 54	77 34 41
58	XXXV	2/71 D	4	Nepâl Himâlaya	24,688	28 32 11	84 05 05
59	Kula Kangri IV	11/77 L	1	Assam Himâlaya	24,660	28 04 11	90 26 53
60	K²⁴	31/52 F	2	Sasir Ridge	24,650	34 48 14	77 48 22
61	K²³	30/52 F	2	Sasir Ridge	24,590	34 50 31	77 47 16
62	Noshaq	Sheet 37 P	..	Hindu Kush	24,573	36 26 06	71 05 08
63	Tirich Mîr II	Sheet 37 P	2	Hindu Kush	24,564	36 15 47	71 49 52
64	Teram Kangri	15/52 E	4	Karakorum	24,489	35 34 38	77 05 04
65	Jonsong	90/78 A	2	Nepâl Himâlaya	24,472	27 52 52	88 08 12
66	Indus-Nagar Watershed No. 2.	46/42 L	2	Haramosh Ridge	24,470	36 00 14	74 52 34
67	Tirich Mîr III	Sheet 37 P	2	Hindu Kush	24,461	36 16 00	71 49 31
68	LVII	116/53 N	3	Kumaun Himâlaya	24,391	30 21 58	79 59 54
69	Muztâgh Ata	7/42 N	2	Muztâgh Ata	24,388	38 16 43 ⎱ 38 ⎰	75 07 06 ⎱ 02 ⎰
70	K¹⁵	8/52 E	4	Karakorum	24,370	35 17 46	77 01 23
71	Close companion of K²³ and K²⁴	48/52 F	..	Sasir Ridge	24,330	34 52 25	77 44 18
72	Kunlun No. 1	3/61 E	2	Kunlun	24,306	35 47 48	81 08 42
73	Ganesh Himal	6/71 H	1	Nepâl Himâlaya	24,299	28 23 30	85 07 45 ⎱ 46 ⎰
74	Kondus	50²/52 A	..	Karakorum	24,280	35 31 06	76 48 07
75	Istor-o-Nal Tirich Mîr IV	Sheet 37 P	2	Hindu Kush	24,271	36 22 38	71 53 52
76	Haramosh	58/43 I	3	Haramosh Ridge	24,270	35 50 29	74 53 52
77	Rimo Peak	51/52 E	2	Karakorum	24,230	35 21 22	77 22 09
78	West Ibi Gamin	48/53 N	..	Zâskâr Range	24,200	30 57 03	79 34 10
79	East Ibi Gamin	Sheet 53 N	..	Zâskâr Range	24,170	30 55 57	79 36 09
80	Churen Himal	4/62 P	7	Nepâl Himâlaya	24,150	28 43 54	83 12 43
81	Sad Ishtrâgh	1/42 D	2	Hindu Kush	24,110	36 32 57	72 06 58
82	Kinjut No. 3	7/42 P	2	Karakorum	24,090	36 19 03	75 02 11 ⎱ 10 ⎰
83	Satellite of Kânchenjunga	6/78 A	2	Nepâl Himâlaya	24,089	27 47 15	88 11 55
84	Nalkankar	Sheet 62 F	..	Nepâl-Tibet Watershed.	24,064	30 17 14	81 23 30
85	Chamlang	42/72 I	2	Nepâl Himâlaya	24,012	27 46 31	86 58 56
86	Kabru	16/78 A	2	Nepâl Himâlaya	24,002	27 36 30	88 06 50

TABLE VI.—Other peaks of more than 24,000 feet, whose positions and heights are not yet sufficiently well known for inclusion in Tables I—V.

Reference Number of Peak.	Name or Symbol.	Peak and Sheet Numbers.	Number of stations from which the height was observed.	System.	Height.	Latitude.	Longitude.
1	2	3	4	5	6	7	8
					feet	° ′ ″	° ′ ″
87	N. E. Satellite of K²	57/52 A	..	Karakorum	24,750	35 55 25	76 33 28
88	N. H. I	Sheet 62 P	2	Nepāl Himālaya	24,509	28 36 50	83 52 25
89	Garmo	Sheet 42 B	..	Trans-Alai Range	24,590	38 56 40	72 01 20
90	Kunjut No. 2	11/42 P	1	Karakorum	24,580	36 12 45	75 15 12
91	Satellite of Kānchenjunga	2/78 A	5	Nepāl Himālaya	24,344	27 52 40	88 08 35
92	Tirich Mīr V	Sheet 37 P	2	Hindu Kush	24,076	36 16 17	71 48 52
93	Hunza-Kunji IV	34/42 L	5	Karakorum	24,044	36 24 10	74 41 43

The question, "what constitutes a peak," has been considered in Chapter 18, Part III, in a reference to the discovery of Teram Kangri. The question, "By whom was Mount Everest discovered?," is considered in Chapter 21, Part III, in a reference to the Nepāl Himālaya.

A column has been included in Tables I to V showing the number of stations from which the height of each peak has been observed. For the attainment of accuracy it is more profitable to observe a peak from different places and distances than to multiply observations from any one station; and the number of observing stations is an indication of the trustworthiness of the resulting value of altitude. The accuracy of the adopted values of height is discussed hereafter and numerical estimates of the magnitudes of the errors that may exist are formed.

A column has also been included showing the Survey of India number and sheet of each peak, in case the reader requires more detailed information.

The latitude and longitude of each peak have been given in the tables, so that its position on the charts may be ascertained. In the drainage Charts XXIV to XXXIV (appended to Part III) these positions have been marked exactly: but in Charts I to V the scale is so small that in crowded clusters there has not been always room to mark the precise position of each peak; a few of the symbols overlapped, and had to be slightly displaced in order to make room for others.

It will be noticed that every peak of Chart I is shown by a larger and larger circle on each of the successive Charts II to V; the reason for this increase is that at the level of 28,000 feet Kānchenjunga, for example, is in nature hardly more than a point, but at 27,000 feet the contour round Kānchenjunga encloses an *area*; and at 24,000 feet a horizontal section taken through the Kānchenjunga pyramid would show that a *considerable* area of the earth's surface had attained that elevation.*

In the fifth column of each table is given the range on which each peak is situated, the great Himālaya range being divided into four sections:—

(i) the Punjab Himālaya from the Indus to the Sutlej;
(ii) the Kumaun Himālaya from the Sutlej to the Kāli;
(iii) the Nepāl Himālaya from the Kāli to the Tīsta;
(iv) the Assam Himālaya from the Tīsta to the Brahmaputra.†

The relative positions of the ranges mentioned in the tables are shown on the range chart which serves as a frontispiece.

Well-known peaks below 24,000 feet.—In Table VII are given the details of a few well-known peaks, which are *less* than 24,000 feet in height. This table unlike the preceding does not contain the names of all peaks above a certain height, and is not therefore a continuation of Table V. Some peaks have been omitted which exceed in height many of those of Table VII; to give complete lists of all known peaks would be to convert this paper into a numerical catalogue.

A great many of the peaks of Table VII are visible from Mussoorie and Landour, and their outlines are shown in Chart VIII.‡ The panorama of Chart VIII is continuous from left to right: it has been drawn in three sections that it might be made to fit the size of this paper. The reference letters A and B have been added to indicate continuity.

TABLE VII.—Some well-known peaks, the heights of which are less than 24,000 feet.

Reference Number of Peak.	Name or Symbol.	Peak and Sheet Numbers.	Number of stations from which the height was observed.	System.	Height.	Latitude.	Longitude.
1	2	3	4	5	6	7	8
					feet	° ′ ″	° ′ ″
94	Api	160/62 B	3	Nepāl Himālaya	23,399	30 00 20	80 55 54
95	Badrināth	27/53 N	5	Kumaun Himālaya	23,190	30 44 16	79 16 52
96	Bandarpūnch	69/53 I	5	Kumaun Himālaya	20,720	31 00 12	78 33 17
97	Chomo Lhāri	38/78 E	2	Assam Himālaya	23,997	27 49 42	89 16 21
98	Chumunko	80/78 A	4	Nepāl Himālaya	17,310	27 27 31	88 47 12
99	Dayabhang	35/71 H	2	Nepāl Himālaya	23,750	28 15 22	85 31 09
100	Deotibba	20/52 H	5	Punjab Himālaya	20,410	32 12 51	77 23 54
101	Dubanni	38/43 I	1	Haramosh Ridge	20,154	35 57 23	74 38 05
102	Dūnagiri	108/53 N	4	Kumaun Himālaya	23,184	30 30 57	79 52 04

* On Chart V peaks of the fifth magnitude have been drawn as points, those of the fourth magnitude have been given a diameter of 6 miles, those of the third a diameter of 12 miles, those of the second a diameter of 18 miles, and those of the first a diameter of 24 miles.

† The Punjab and Kumaun Himālaya have been for the most part surveyed; the peaks of the Nepāl Himālaya have been observed from long distances and the country was topographically surveyed in 1924: the Assam Himālaya form still a *terra incognita*, although many of the peaks have been well observed from the south, and surveys of an exploratory nature have been carried out in 1911-13 and 1921-22.

‡ This chart was copied from the panorama drawn by Col. St. G. C. Gore, C.S.I., R.E., in 1887.

TABLE VII.—Some well-known peaks, the heights of which are less than 24,000 feet—contd.

Reference Number of Peak.	Name or Symbol.	Peak and Sheet Numbers.	Number of stations from which the height was observed.	System.	Height.	Latitude.	Longitude.
1	2	3	4	5	6	7	8
					feet	° ′ ″	° ′ ″
103	Gangotri*	11/53 J	3	Kumaun Himalaya	21,700	30 52 58	78 52 14
104	Gardhâr	13/52 D	1	Punjab Himalaya	21,140	32 55 07	76 42 48
105	Gauri Sankar†	6/72 I	6	Nepal Himalaya	23,440	27 57 52	86 20 16
106	Gyala Peri	Sheet 82 K	..	Assam Himalaya	23,460	29 48 52	94 59 05
107	Jaonli	17/53 J	1	Kumaun Himalaya	21,760	30 51 17	78 51 25
108	Jibjibia East ‡	57/71 H	2	Nepal Himalaya	21,839	28 07 41	85 52 16
109	Jibjibia West ‡	55/71 H	2	Nepal Himalaya	22,876	28 10 25	83 46 51
110	Kailās	Sheet 62 E	2	Kailās	22,028	31 04 02	81 18 50
111	Kaufmann	Sheet 42 A	..	Trans-Alai	23,000	39 18 20	72 50 03
112	Kedârnâth	7/53 N	6	Kumaun Himalaya	22,770	30 47 53	79 04 07
113	Kharchakund	8/53 N	1	Kumaun Himalaya	21,695	30 46 46	79 07 47
114	Kungpu	36/78 E	..	Assam Himalaya	22,252	27 50 46	89 20 16
115	Lunkho	Sheet 42 D	2	Hindu Kush	22,641	36 46 36	72 26 16
116	Mer or Kānaṣ	7/52 B	2	Punjab Himalaya	23,250	34 00 48	76 03 22
117	Muztāgh	1/61 A	..	Kunlun	23,890	35 56 21	80 14 10
118	Nampa	Sheet 62 F	4	Nepal Himalaya	22,162	30 00 37	81 00 03
119	Nandakna	76/53 N	2	Kumaun Himalaya	20,700	30 20 56	79 43 09
120	Nandakot	41/62 B	3	Kumaun Himalaya	22,510	30 16 51	80 04 11
121	Narsing	44/78 A	4	Nepal Himalaya	19,130	27 30 40	88 17 02
122	Nilakanta	28/53 N	3	Kumaun Himalaya	21,640	30 43 52	79 24 28
123	Nodzinkangsa	1/77 L	..	Nepāl-Tibet Watershed.	23,794	28 57 16	90 11 33
124	Nyenchen-tang-lha	5/77 J	3	Nyenchen-tang-lha.	23,255	30 22 17	90 35 18
125	Panch Chūlhi	92/62 B	3	Kumaun Himalaya	22,650	30 12 51	80 25 41
126	Pandim	18/78 A	8	Nepāl Himalaya	22,010	27 34 38	88 13 10
127	Pauhunri	69/78 A	2	Nepāl Himalaya	23,180	27 56 56	88 50 39
128	Riwo Phargyul North ‡	39/53 I	2	Zāskār	22,210	31 54 08	78 44 39
129	Riwo Phargyul South ‡	41/53 I	2	Zāskār	22,170	31 53 05	78 44 05
130	Sargaroin	64/53 I	2	Kumaun Himalaya	20,370	31 06 08	78 30 04
131	Ser or Nāna§	1/52 C	6	Punjab Himalaya	23,410	33 58 56	76 01 31
132	Simvo	14/78 A	2	Nepāl Himalaya	22,360	27 40 44	88 14 38
133	Srikānta	7/53 J	4	Kumaun Himalaya	20,120	30 57 25	78 48 22
134	Tengri Khān	Sheet 11, Chinese Turkistān and Kansu.	..	Tien Shan	23,600	42 24 10	80 16 46
135	Tharlasagar	14/53 J	2	Kumaun Himalaya	22,610	30 51 41	78 59 45
136	Trisūl East	121/53 N	4	Kumaun Himalaya	22,320	30 16 14	79 52 24
137	Trisūl West	117/53 N	7	Kumaun Himalaya	23,360	30 18 43	79 46 40

*The twin of Jaonli. ‖The twin of Mer. ‡Twins.
†Double-peaked. §The twin of Ser.

A SINGLE PEAKED SUMMIT

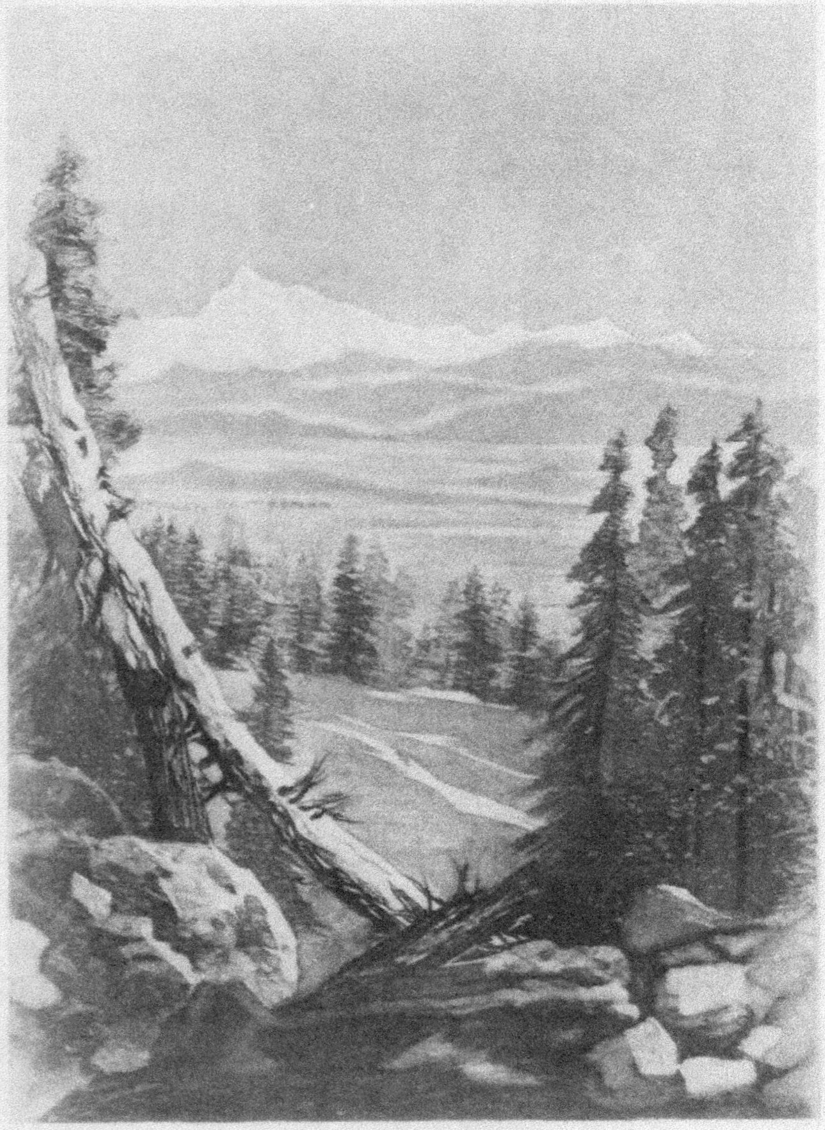

NANGA PARBAT

AS SEEN FROM A DISTANCE OF [illegible] MILES

From a photograph by Colonel George Strahan R.E.

A DOUBLE PEAKED SUMMIT

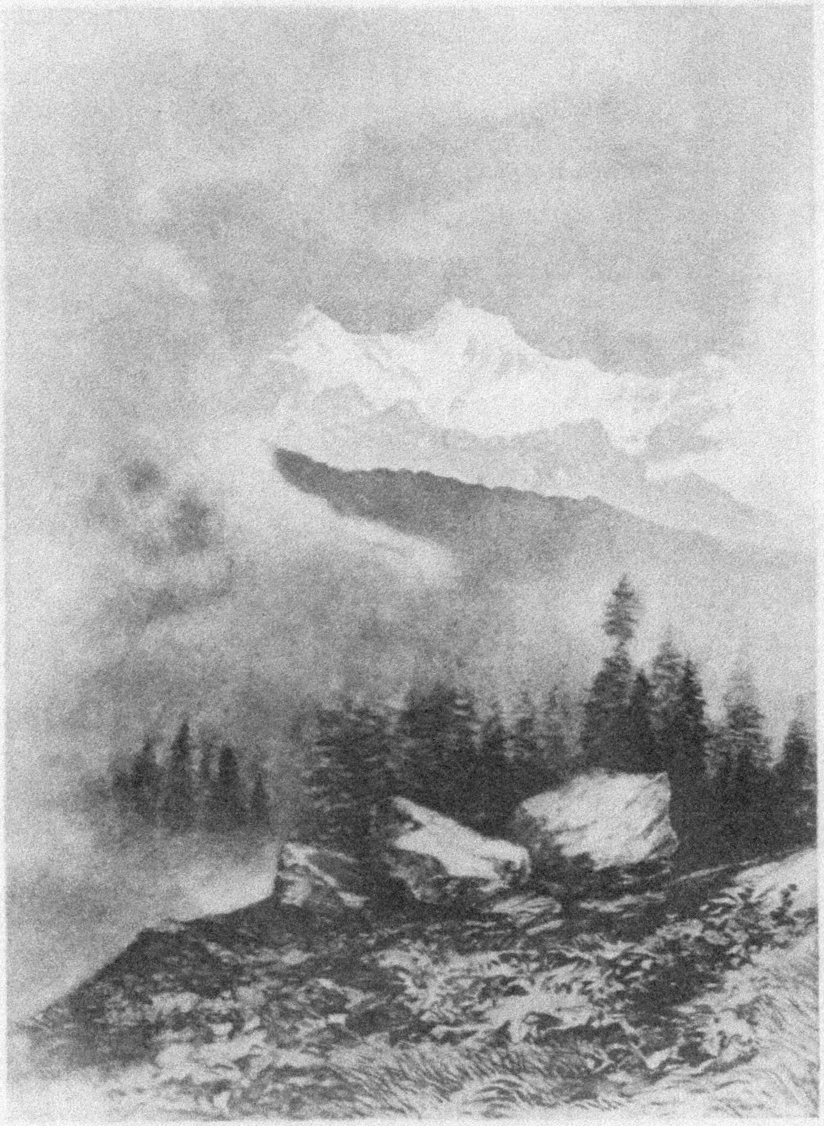

BANDAR PUNCH

AS SEEN FROM A DISTANCE OF [illegible] MILES

From a photograph by Colonel George Strahan R.E.

CHAPTER 2

THE EVOLUTION OF GEOGRAPHICAL NAMES IN THE HIMĀLAYA.

The ancient monuments of India are preserved by the Archaeological Survey; they tell us of the history and arts and thoughts of peoples who lived and died in bye-gone epochs. The Survey of India has in its keeping similar monuments of the past in the shape of geographical names. Ancient buildings and coins appeal to us through our sight and our touch, ancient names impress us by their sound and harmony with their surroundings.

Names such as Himālaya and Kailās are ancient monuments that bear comparison with the stone pillars of Asoka and with the ruins of Ayodhya and Delhi. Names like Gangotri and Badrīnāth are reminders of the courage and enterprise of the Aryan pilgrims who were the first explorers to penetrate the Himālayan gorges and passes. The nomenclature of the Himālayan basin of the Ganges, with its rivers and shrines and peaks and towns, is a remarkable example of Sanskrit art. The name Indus is a relic of the Persian invasion of India in the reign of Darius the Great, 24 centuries ago. The name Hindu Kush has come down to us from Alexander the Great. The name Takht-i-Sulaimān was probably brought to India from Samarkand by one of the Mughal emperors.

Languages are the basis of geographical names, and languages have their origin in history; and thus it is that geography and language and history are all parts of one whole.

Every geographer in countries like Kashmīr, or Western Tibet, or Nepāl or Sikkim, where different races and religions are in contact, finds it necessary to understand the histories of the peoples. Some such knowledge is required to enable him to escape from the bewilderment with which his mind becomes oppressed; without such knowledge he is unable to apply the advice of travellers or linguists to the uses of geography. Before dealing, therefore, with questions of nomenclature I am introducing here a brief outline of historical events that either have, or may have influenced the geographical names. This outline is divided into two tables, one for the Western Himālaya and the western half of Tibet, the other for the Eastern Himālaya and Eastern Tibet.

Historical Table showing the dates of important events in history which may have influenced the nomenclature of the Western Himālaya and Western Tibet.

3000 to 2000 B.C.—Invasion of India by the Aryans who migrated from Persia through Afghānistān. Mongolians from China settle in Western Tibet.

1500 B.C.—In the Mahābhārata and the Rāmāyana references are made to many geographical names such as Kailās, Sindhu, Mānasarowar, Kasmira.

570 B.C.—The doctrines of Buddhism are preached in India.

521 B.C. (The Persian Empire).—The conquest of the Punjab by the Persians under Darius the Great. The names Indostan, Hindu, Indus (corruption of the Sanskrit Sindhu) date from the Persian Empire.

450 B.C.—Herodotus mentions Tibetans established in Western Tibet, and Dards in Gilgit. The Afghān name Pathān has been traced in Herodotus (Stein).

327 B.C. (The Greek Empire).—The Greek invasion of India under Alexander the Great. The Greeks adopted many Sanskrit names, but changed their pronunciations and spellings.

321 B.C.—Chandragupta King of the Punjab.

260 B.C. (The Buddhist Empire).—The Empire of Asoka extends over India and Afghānistān.

240 B.C. to 600 A.D.—Buddhism spreads from India into Tibet: Kailās and Mānasarowar, sacred to the Aryans, became sacred to the Tibetans.

997 to 1007 A.D.—Invasions of India by Mahmūd of Ghazni. Arab geographers begin to visit India.

1200 A.D. (The Mongol Empire).—Gengkis Khan founds the Mongol empire, with his capital at Karakorum; he conquers Central and Western Asia and invades India.

1294 A.D.—Hindu rulers of Kashmīr are replaced by Muhammadan.

1332 to 1342 A.D.—Ibn Batūta visits India, and writes his travels.

1398 A.D. (The Tartar Empire).—Invasion of India and Kashmīr by the Amīr Tīmūr.

1526 A.D. (The Mughal Empire).—The Mughal Empire of Delhi is founded by the Emperor Bābar, who was descended from both Gengkis Khan and Tīmūr.

Muhammadan writers introduce many modern Persian names: these must not be confused with the old Persian names that date from Darius.

1531 A.D.—Mirza Muhammad Haidar at the head of a Muhammadan army from Kāshgar crosses the Karakorum pass, conquers Little Tibet and invades Kashmīr.

1586 A.D.—Muhammadan rulers of Kashmīr are replaced by the Emperor Akbar.

1600 A.D.—The Dards (Aryans) of Gilgit-Hunza and the Tibetans of Balti become Muhammadans. The countries then become known by the Persian names Dardistân and Baltistān.

1756 A.D.—Kashmīr conquered by the Afghāns under Ahmad Shāh Durrāni.

1819 A.D.—Kashmīr conquered by Ranjīt Singh, the Sikh monarch.

1845 A.D.—Gulāb Singh, Mahārāja of Jammu and Kashmīr and leader of the Dogras, conquers Ladākh, a Buddhist province subject to Lhāsa; a year later he annexes Baltistān.

1857 A.D.—Geographical interest becomes focussed upon Western Tibet by Colonel Montgomerie's discovery that the second highest mountain in the world is situated there.

Historical Table showing the dates of important events in history which may have influenced the nomenclature of the Eastern Himālaya and Eastern Tibet.

2000 B.C.—Migrations of Mongolians from China flow over Tibet and into the higher valleys of the Himālaya.

2000 B.C.—Another Mongolian migration from North Burma and Tibet penetrates the Assam Himālaya and the hills of Bhutān, Sikkim and Nepāl.

640 A.D.—Buddhism is definitely accepted by Tibet. Shrines sacred to the Hindus "like Gauri Sankar and Gosainthān" become sacred also to the Tibetans. Tibetan shrines become goals of pilgrimage for Chinese and other Buddhist races.

750 A.D.—Guru Padma the Sanskrit scholar was called from India by the King of Tibet.

800 A.D.—Tibet at war with China.

1250 A.D.—The Mongol empire of Karakorum is extended over Tibet.

1350 A.D.—Rājputs from Rājputāna subdue the Newârs of Nepāl.

1559 A.D.—The Rājputs conquer the town of Gorka in Nepāl.

1700 A.D.—Chinese suzerainty begins in Tibet.

1711 A.D.—First Chinese surveys of Tibet; they gave to geography the names Kentaisse and Chumalhari.

1769 A.D.—The Gurkha Prithwī Nārāyan becomes ruler of Nepāl.

1788 A.D.—Gurkhas from Nepāl invade Sikkim.

1790 A.D.—A Gurkha army invades Tibet.

1792 A.D.—A Chinese army invades Nepāl.

1850 A.D.—The discovery is made by the Survey of India that the highest mountain in the world is situated in the unexplored region separating Tibet from Nepāl.

In tracing the advances of geographical knowledge that have been gained in the high mountains of Asia, a narrator feels impelled to refer to the untimely deaths of explorers like Moorcroft, of surveyors like Basevi, of geologists like Stoliezka, of mountaineers like Mallory, but the task is beyond him. No such record would be just unless it showed the names of their assistants and khalāsis and coolies who have died in the same cause. And even then the list would be limited to our own short age, and would be ignoring the numerous sacrifices of life that must have been made when the sources of the Ganges were first explored by pilgrims.

The Linguistic Survey of India.

In 1927 the volumes of the Linguistic Survey of India were published; they dealt with 179 different languages and 544 different dialects. They were written by Sir George Grierson, an officer of the Indian Civil Service, who had devoted fifty years to this work, and who had been in touch with all the oriental linguists of his time. In the mountains of India, Afghānistān and Tibet there are in use among the peoples 70 different languages and dialects, all of which are dealt with in Grierson's work. As time goes on, the knowledge collected by the Linguistic Survey will become of value to the geographical survey; the new volumes will enable geographers to understand much that was obscure to their predecessors; many of our difficulties will be explained, and many causes of confusion will be removed. As an Appendix to Part I of this Himālayan Geography I have added a synopsis of the Linguistic Survey.

Throughout the Himālayas, Tibet, Pāmirs, and Afghānistān there are no Semitic or Dravidian languages. All the languages of these mountainous countries, with one small exception, belong either to the Aryan or to the Mongolian family. The one exception is Burushaski, an ancient language still spoken in parts of Hunza; Sir George Grierson was unable to classify Burushaski with any one of the great linguistic families. (Burushaski was called Khajunah by Sir Alexander Cunningham in his book *Ladak*, 1854. Colonel Lorimer, who is the authority on the Shina language, is now publishing a book on Burushaski.)

About 3000 B.C. two different races, the Aryan and the Mongolian, began to move towards one another and to converge upon India and Tibet, the Aryans migrating from Persia, the Mongolians from China. They eventually settled down in contact, and their ethnographic boundary can still be traced. In the Western Himālayas (Kashmīr) the well-known pass Zoji La is described by Grierson as "the ethnographic watershed between the Aryan and Tibetan populations." In the Eastern Himālayas (Assam and Bhutān) the Mongolian peoples have occupied all the higher and lower valleys and the outer hills, and the interracial boundary skirts the plains. From Kashmīr to Bhutān the ethnographic boundary between Aryan and Mongolian follows an irregular line through Spiti, Garhwāl, Nepāl and Sikkim, the Aryans now occupying all the Himālayan hills on the Indian side of this line, the Mongolians living on the Tibetan side. As the centuries have passed, the Aryan peoples living in the mountains have become separated into many distinct branches, the Dards of Gilgit and Hunza, the Kashmīris, Garhwālis, Kumaunis and Nepāl Pahāris, but all these races have come from the main Aryan stock. The Mongolian advance from China was composed of three separate migrations: a Tibeto-Burman branch came through Northern Burma into the Assam hills, another Tibeto-Burman branch moved from the sources of the Irrawaddy across Southern Tibet into the higher valleys of the Himālayas behind Nepāl and Kumaun. The third migration consisted of the ancestors of the present Tibetan race: they came from China and settled in Tibet: their settlements extended as far west as Baltistān, and into the higher Himālayan valleys. The Tibeto-Burmans now constitute a long series of tribes separating the Aryans from the pure Tibetans, in Sikkim, Nepāl and Kumaun. The Tibeto-Burman dialects spoken in the Himālayas form a linguistic chain connecting the Tibetan language with the Burmese.

Sir George Grierson writes (in a letter dated February 27th, 1931),

"There can be no doubt that many Tibeto-Burman languages along the southern face "of the Himālaya originally came over the passes from the north. Before the Aryan invasion "the south face of the Himālaya was inhabited by speakers of Munda languages. Then came "the Aryan invasion from the north-west, and the Tibeto-Burman infiltration from the north, "so that nowadays the south face of the Himālaya presents a very curious mixture of languages."

CHAPTER 3.

GEOGRAPHICAL NAMES THAT HAVE GIVEN RISE TO CONTROVERSY.

(1) The principle followed by the Survey of India has been to accept for geography only such names as are in common use by the inhabitants of the country. There have been two exceptions to this rule, in which cases the scientific requirements of geography have outweighed local considerations. The two exceptions are :—
  (a) *Mount Everest*, which was the name given to the highest mountain of the world in 1865.
  (b) *Trans-Himālaya*, which was the name given by Sven Hedin to the great mountainous region of Central Tibet in 1908, and which was adopted by the Survey of India in 1931.

(2) The geographical outlook of the Tibetans and Mongols is local : they name their passes and grazing-grounds and water, but not their long ranges. The three following names have been borrowed (one from a province and two from peaks) and have been attached by the Survey to mountain ranges— Ladākh, Kailās, Muztāgh Ata.

  (a) *Ladākh Range*—this name belonged originally to the province of Western Tibet ; it was given by Godwin-Austen in 1884 to the mountain range of Ladākh : the Survey of India unable to devise a better name has adopted the name "Ladākh range," but it has not proved altogether satisfactory, as the mountain range has been found to extend beyond the limits of Ladākh both on the northwest and south-east.

  (b) *Kailās Range*—Kailās is the name of a sacred peak situated upon a mountain range. In 1820 this name was extended along the range by Moorcroft for fifty miles from the peak. In 1829, Dr. Gerard wrote of "the great "Kylas chain." The name was extended along the same range to a still further distance from the Kailās mountain in 1854 by Cunningham. The ranges of Tibet are long, and any names given to them are liable to require extension. The extension of the name Kailās to a great distance from the Kailās mountain has not been satisfactory. If Kailās had not been so well-known the transference of its name to a long range would have been less objectionable, but Kailās happens to be the best known peak in Asia, and the name is out of place in Western Tibet. The name "Kailās Range" is now, however, well established and there has been no desire on the part of geographers to see it altered. I only refer to the disadvantages of extending the name of the peak to the range, that they may be considered when a similar case arises in future.

  (c) The name "*Muztāgh Ata Range*" was given by Stein to the range bordering the Takla Makān desert on the west. Stein took this name from the peak Muztāgh Ata. The range had already been named the Muztāgh Range by Sven Hedin in 1890 (*Through Asia, p. 670*), and had been called by Wauhope the Muztāgh Range in 1906. Stein's name Muztāgh Ata is more distinctive in Turkistān than Muztāgh, and as the Muztāgh Ata range is a relatively short range compared with those traversing Tibet, there will be no reasons for extending the name Muztāgh Ata to such great distances from the peak as have proved inconvenient in the case of Kailās.

(3) The inhabitants of high mountain countries occasionally transfer the names of passes to the ranges, and this is a better system than the transference of a provincial name like Ladākh or of a peak-name like Kailās. When an Asiatic traveller is asked the name of the mountains he has crossed, it is only natural that he should give the name of the pass.

The traveller regards the range as an impediment to his progress, and the pass as a means of surmounting that impediment: the Rattan Pīr pass provides the way by which the Rattan Pīr range can be passed. The following ranges named after passes are believed to have been given their names by Asiatic travellers :—

(1) Pīr Panjāl Range, south of Kashmīr. (Authority—Drew's *Jammu and Kashmīr*, p. 78.)
(2) Rattan Pīr Range, south of Kashmīr. (Drew.)
(3) Karo La in Southern Tibet. (Ryder.)
(4) Karakorum ⎫ both these names were probably taken from the passes
(5) Muztāgh   ⎭ by wayfarers and attached to the range of Western Tibet.
(6) Hattoo Pīr near Nanga Parbat. (General Bruce.)
(7) Bhairav in Nepāl. (Hodgson.)
(8) Langur in Nepāl, used by Jesuits for a mountain, and by Hodgson for a pass. (Hedin's *Southern Tibet*, Vol. III, p. 104.)
(9) The name Chomo Lungma may have been taken by Sharpa Bhotias from the pass Lungma La, and extended to the mountain region above the pass.

THE GEOGRAPHICAL MEANING OF THE WORD "TIBET".

The highland of Tibet consists of many different tablelands separated by mountain chains. There is no other elevation upon the earth's surface that can be compared with Tibet, and there is consequently no word in geography that describes the protuberant mass of Tibet.

In 1888, Sir Richard Strachey wrote (*Encyclopaedia Britannica, 1888*), "Geographers were convinced of the physical unity of the mountainous region "which extends from longitude 74° to 95°. Tibet is a protuberance above the "general level of the earth's surface, of which the Himālaya and the Kunlun "are the southern and northern borders."

From the earliest times, Tibet has been divided by geographers into Great Tibet and Little Tibet. Great Tibet consists of the central and eastern regions of the highland, and Little Tibet has been the name given to Baltistān. The two names are used in the Āīn-i-Akbari: and Bernier describes the interview of the King of Little Tibet with the Emperor Aurangzeb in Kashmīr. In 1788 Rennell showed both names on his map, and in 1854 Henry Strachey found the two terms in use amongst Tibetans. In his Survey of Western Tibet, 1855-1865, Colonel Montgomerie entered the name "Little Tibet" on his maps, and it is still to be seen on the maps of the Survey of India. This name has a historic tradition behind it, and it should certainly be preserved in geography. Its presence on the maps emphasises the important truth that Baltistān forms part of Tibet.

It would perhaps have not been necessary to discuss here the geographical meaning of Tibet had it not been for a difference of opinion that arose in 1930. In June of that year, a paper was read before the Royal Society upon "the "Geographical Representation of the Mountains of Tibet," and it dealt particularly with the alignment of the Karakorum mountains from western to central Tibet (*Proceedings of the Royal Society, Series A, Vol. 127, June 2nd 1930*). In the following August the editor of the "Geographical Journal" in criticising this paper contended that it could not refer to Ladākh, or to the Karakorum mountains of Baltistān, because it was referring to Tibet and to the Tibetan population. He went on to say that Colonel Montgomerie, who made the surveys of Ladākh and Baltistān, "was not concerned at all with Tibet."* These statements unaccompanied by any explanation could only mean that Ladākh and Baltistān are not parts of Tibet and that their populations are not Tibetan. The question is one of scientific importance. The editor has been confusing geographical Tibet with political Tibet, and such confusion can be avoided if due regard is paid to the context. Geographical Tibet embraces the whole highland protuberance stretching, as Richard Strachey said, from longitude 74° to 95°, and including Ladākh and Baltistān. Political Tibet denotes the country under the Government of Lhāsa; the political boundary of Kashmīr separates Ladākh and Baltistān from Tibet.

Geographers are not responsible for this difficulty and they have to meet it with understanding. The mountain mass was named Tibet long before political boundaries came into existence. The Arab Istakhri mentioned Tibet in 590 A.D. Ibn Khurdaba mentioned it in 880 A.D., and Marco Polo used the name. In 1820 Ladākh was under Lhāsa, and Moorcroft the first European explorer, regarded it as part of Tibet. The difference between geographical and political Tibet was introduced in 1846, when the Mahārāja of Jammu and Kashmīr annexed Ladākh and Baltistān. The annexation did not alter the physical unity of the protuberant mass of Tibet, nor did it affect the ethnographic boundary of the Tibetan race.

---

*Compare Sven Hedin, Southern Tibet, Vol. VII, p. 208, "Montgomerie, the greatest authority of his time on Western Tibet."

In 1854 Henry Strachey wrote as follows, "The north-west extremity of "all Tibet comprises the modern provinces of Ladākh and Baltistān. I consider "Tibet to be terminated by the southward turn of the Indus towards India."

In 1888 Sir Henry Yule wrote, "Tibet is the vast and lofty tableland of "which the Himālaya forms the southern marginal range, and which may be "said roughly to extend from the Indus elbow north-west of Kashmīr to the "borders of China."

In 1907 the Rev. Francke wrote the "History of Western Tibet"; it is a history of Ladākh and Baltistān. Francke lived for many years in Khalatse on the Indus, and he has been the great authority on the Balti language. In his history, he writes that "the political boundary between western Tibet and "central Tibet is the Lahri stream near the Pengong lake." Strachey's definition of Tibet has been hitherto accepted by geographical authorities, from Sir Clement Markham to Sven Hedin.

When the editor of the "Geographical Journal" denies that the population living south of the Karakorum range in Baltistān and Ladākh is Tibetan, his view conflicts with the ethnological authorities; and this question of the population is not even dependent upon the political boundary. That the Ladākhis and Baltīs are Tibetan was shown by Cunningham in his book on Ladākh, 1854; it was clearly shown by Drew in his race map of 1875; it has been corroborated by Grierson in his Linguistic Survey of India, 1927; he writes, "the Zoji "La Pass is the ethnographic watershed between the Aryan and Tibetan "populations."

In the latest edition, 1930, of the Encyclopaedia Britannica, under the article Ladākh the following explanation of Tibet is given:—

"The adjoining territory of Baltistān forms the west extremity of Tibet, whose natural "limits here are the Indus (from its abrupt southward bend in Long. 74° 45′ E.) and the moun-"tains to the north and west separating a peaceful Tibetan population from the fiercer Aryan "tribes. The ethnological frontier of Tibet coincides with the geographical one."

The Imperial Gazetteer regards Baltistān as part of Ladākh, but includes both in Tibet. It says, "Ladākh is the most westerly province of the high "mountainous land spoken of as Tibet. The Karakorum range forms the north-"ern boundary as far east as the Karakorum Pass,........Baltistān is known as "Little Tibet."

In the case of every important mountain alignment of the world, a single name has been used throughout its length to show its physical unity. It would be a mistake to limit the name Tibet to the political boundary and to separate the western end of the highland from the central portion. Geography forms a basis for geology and meteorology, and these sciences are concerned with the Tibetan highland as a whole.

Mr. Sherring's work on "Western Tibet and the British Borderland" is clearly referring to political Tibet: Mr. Francke's history of "Western Tibet" clearly refers to geographical Tibet. If the two meanings of the name Tibet are found in the future to be inconvenient (and this has not happened hitherto) it will possibly be advantageous to retain the name Tibet for geographical purposes and to accept the name Bodyul for the country governed from Lhāsa. Sir George Grierson writes (*Linguistic Survey, III (1), 14*). "Tibetans call their "country Bodyul, and their language Bodskad; a Tibetan is Bodpa."

Many writers have experienced a difficulty in deciding whether to describe Tibet as a tableland or as a plateau: it consists of many tablelands and many plateaux. In 1886 Sir Henry Yule wrote, "Objections have been raised to "the application of the word tableland to so rugged a region of inequalities, but "it is a technical expression in geography applicable to a large area which is at "all parts at a considerable height above sea-level." Yule, however, quotes with sympathy the British soldier who said in Abyssinia, "Call this a tableland? "then it's a table with the legs uppermost."

During the last half century, geographers seem gradually to have been adopting the British soldier's view in preference to Yule's. There is now a growing tendency in writers to refer to Tibet as a highland.

The meaning of the word Bhotia.

In the last century there was a belief in the Survey of India that Bhotiās, some of whom had taken service in the Survey, belonged to a race intermediate between the Aryan and the Tibetan. But ethnologists have shown that there is no such intermediate race. In 1854 Sir Alexander Cunningham, who knew the districts of Lahoul and Spiti, wrote "Bhotiās are a branch of the great "Mongolian race."

Mr. C. A. Sherring of the Indian Civil Service in his book on "Western "Tibet and the British Borderland," 1906, has given a description of the Bhotiās of Kumaun: "The Bhotiās are of Tibetan origin," he writes, "though they "themselves have the belief that they were originally Hindus." Sherring also says that the Bhotiās are becoming Hinduised, that they add Singh to their names, and that whilst some understand the Tibetan language, others speak Tibeto-Burman dialects.

The following quotation is from Atkinson's Gazetteer of the Himālayan Districts, 1886, Vol. III:—"It cannot be doubted that the Bhotiyas are of "Tibetan origin. They do not admit their Tibetan origin. They state they are "a Rājput race who dwelt originally in the hill provinces south of the snowy "range, and that they migrated to Tibet whence after a residence of several "generations they again crossed the Himālaya and established themselves in the "districts which they now inhabit. The Bhotiyas have however lived so long "amongst and mingled so much with the Tibetans that they possess no claim to "be recognised as of Indian origin. All Bhotiyas unite in assumptions of superi- "ority to the natives of Tibet."

Sir George Grierson does not enter upon ethnological questions: he writes only from the linguistic point of view. He says that Bhotia means Tibetan, a Bhotia is a Tibetan, and that the Bhotia language is the Tibetan language.

General Bruce in his book "Twenty Years in the Himālaya," refers to Sharpa Bhotiās. Grierson states that a Sharpa Bhotia is a Tibetan who is living in Nepāl.

The Name Trans-Himālaya.

Trans-Himālaya was the name given by Sven Hedin to the high mountain region of Central Tibet which he discovered and explored in 1906-08. It had been believed prior to 1906 that long mountain ranges traversed Tibet from west to east. It had been known too that the Karakorum and Kailās ranges which were compressed together in Western Tibet were diverging widely from one another further east, but since the exploration of Nain Singh in 1875 it had been conjectured that the space between these ranges would consist principally of plateau land. The discovery by Sven Hedin that an interior zone of Tibet, 100 miles in width and stretching from longitude 80° to 90°, was a labyrinth of high mountains came as a surprise. The Himālayan range and the Ladākh range had been traced by geographers as curved alignments of high peaks from west to east, but Trans-Himālaya had no such marked crest-line. Its high points did not follow any linear arrangement, and Sven Hedin was thus unable to call it a range. He named this area Trans-Himālaya.

The discovery of Trans-Himālaya has raised the scientific problem of its relationship to the Karakorum range on the north and to the Kailās range on the south. It has also given rise to a difficult problem of nomenclature. When Sven Hedin arrived in Simla from Tibet in 1908, he gave a public address upon his explorations and he announced his intention of designating the newly discovered mountains of Central Tibet by the name of Trans-Himālaya. His lecture was published in the newspapers of India. It is difficult for a reading public to appreciate the details of new and complicated explorations, but it is easy for them to grasp the significance of a new name. They were less interested in the discussion on mountains than they were in the new name. This was very unfortunate. Sven Hedin's explorations had been so arduous and so important that they deserved cordial and generous recognition, but public opinion in India took exception to the name Trans-Himālaya. It would have been better if Sven Hedin had allowed his geographical discoveries to be slowly appreciated and understood, before he had introduced the name Trans-Himālaya. A geographical name is not only a matter of scientific convenience; it has also its sentimental and artistic sides. The Survey of India and the public in India held the view that the mountains of Central Tibet ought to be given a Tibetan name; they thought it unfair to force an Indian name with a Latin prefix upon the Tibetan people. In the case of Mount Everest, the mountain was standing not in Tibet, but on the Nepāl-Tibet boundary and had been fixed from India. Trans-Himālaya was in the middle of Tibet.

Twenty-three years have now passed since Sven Hedin found his new name opposed in India. The necessity of finding a scientific name for the Trans-Himālayan region of Tibet has of late years become urgent. Frequent endeavours have been made to find a Tibetan name, but they have all ended in disappointment. Tibetan scholars and travellers have been consulted, but none has been able to suggest the ideal name that has been awaited. The Survey of India has thus been led to recognise the force of Sven Hedin's arguments, and to accept the name Trans-Himālaya which he introduced.

Sven Hedin's great work "Southern Tibet", published in 1917 in nine volumes with numerous maps and panoramas, constitutes in itself a complete library of Tibetan geography. Throughout the course of these volumes the student's admiration is aroused both by the accurate, painstaking research and by the fairness and generosity with which the exploratory surveys of all former geographers have been combined together into one geographical history. Sven Hedin writes; "I have done my best not to forget or overlook a single traveller "or scholar from the remotest times to our own days",—and this claim is completely justified. Volume I opens with a generously-worded dedication to the Survey of India, and Volume IV gives an account of Trans-Himālaya and of the orographical problems which its discovery has presented.

The Hindu Kush.

The origin of the foreign name Hindu Kush for the mountain range of Afghānistān has been a source of controversy. Ibn Batūta, the Muhammadan traveller, wrote in 1334 A.D.;—"The mountain is called Hindu Kush because "so many slaves, male and female, brought from India die on the passage of "this mountain owing to the severe cold and snow." Sir Aurel Stein has expressed his disagreement with Ibn Batūta's explanation.

In 1504 the Emperor Bābar wrote in his Memoirs, "Between Balkh and "Kabul is interposed the mountain Hindu Kush, the passes over which are seven "in number."

In 1793 Major Rennell, Surveyor General of Bengal, explained that the term Hindu Kush was probably a corruption of the name Indian Caucasus used by the Greeks during the invasion of India by Alexander the Great, and by Greek historians. Sir Henry Yule agreed with Rennell.

In 1904 in his book "India" Sir Thomas Holdich wrote that the Hindu Kush chain owed its name to the fact that a Hindu force was lost in its attempt to cross into Turkistān by a pass now known as the "Dead Hindu." In 1931 Rennell's explanation is generally accepted.

The question has been raised at times whether the Hindu Kush should be regarded as one range or two; it has two parallel crest-lines. Sir Thomas Holdich wrote in 1906, "The Afghāns regard the Hindu Kush as one mountain "range, but geographers regard it as two. The proximity and parallelism of the "two ranges certainly lead us to think that both are parts of one upheaval. "Geologists have told me that a wide flat-topped range, as the Hindu Kush "originally was, frequently has its top composed of softer rock than its walls "and that the soft top becomes excavated by drainage; a longitudinal river "thus becomes developed between the two walls, and these latter then appear "as separate ranges."

Mount Everest.

The name Mount Everest is now firmly established and definitely adopted: there is no question of changing it ("*Mount Everest: The Reconnaissance,*" *1921: page 13*). But the controversies over the various local names that have been suggested for the mountain have an historic interest. Such controversies are apt to recur, and it is useful to surveyors who find themselves involved in them to know how their predecessors acted and to what extent the decisions taken in the past have been justified by time. There are, moreover other reasons why these controversies should be recorded in a Survey book. The Survey of India is meeting with difficulties in the geographical nomenclature of Tibet, and the sidelights thrown upon the general question by local controversies are often illuminating. There are difficulties in Tibetan nomenclature that have not been encountered in Afghānistān or in Burma. Survey names require to be fixed, but Tibetan names are often vague and cloudlike. The spelling of survey names is based upon pronunciation, but Tibetan names are not spelt in accordance with pronunciation. Another difficulty arises from books of ritual and the writings of Lāmas. These books vaguely refer to mystic geographical names and the latter are quoted by linguists. Geographers, however, cannot accept them until they have found them in use amongst an influential section of the local population. There are in Tibetan literature thirteen different names for the river Ganges, but they are not in local use. Two English sportsmen who crossed the Jelukhaga Pass into Tibet in 1911 were accompanied by Tibetans through all the high valleys of the Himālayas. They found that the Indian river names Bhāgīrathi and Jadhganga were used by the Tibetans, even amongst themselves, for the tributaries of the Ganges. The Lāmas who made the map of Tibet in 1711 showed geographical names which are not in modern use. Mr. Van Manen learnt of six names applied in a book of Tibetan ritual to the six peaks surrounding Mount Everest, but they were subsequently found to agree with the six names that Colonel Morshead had heard applied by Tibetans to the peaks of Gauri Sankar. If it had not been for the accident that Morshead, linguist and surveyor, had visited Gauri Sankar, the Survey might have been pressed to apply the names to Mount Everest: and our position would have been a weak one, for the book of ritual seemed unanswerable. Mr. Macdonald learnt from an official at Lhāsa that the Tibetan name of Mount Everest is Mi-ti Gu-ti Cha-pu Tong-nga, but this name was not heard by the Mount Everest expeditions.—See Sir Charles Bell's letter, page 12, *Professional Paper No. 26, Survey of India*, 1931.

Sarat Chandra Das gives in his dictionary (p. 450) Jomo-Gans-Dkar as "a Tibetan name for Mount Everest." Sarat Chandra did not hear the name locally applied to Mount Everest: he learnt it in Lhāsa. The name is not known locally. Ryder and Wood, when viewing Mount Everest from South Tibet, did not hear it. The probable meaning of this name, like that of others, is that it is "a Tibetan name that might be suitable for a high mountain, if any "name for it was wanted."

The Lāma of Rongbuk Monastery (near Mount Everest) has recently written his biography, which may in future be quoted as a geographical authority. Mr. Van Manen has kindly translated page 46: "In the southern part of La-stod "there is the interior part of Phaduk Gyarnorong where there is a mountain called "Jomo-Langma which is the place of religious practice of Mi-gyo-glang-bzang-ma, "who is one of the five sisters Tshering-chenga." Can this sentence be regarded as evidence that Jomo Langma is the Tibetan name for Mount Everest? The Lāma says that Jomo Langma is a place of religious practice: the other geographic names he mentions belong to the peaks of Gauri Sankar (*Survey of India, Professional Paper No. 26, 1931: p. 9*).

The Lāma does not himself regard his biography as a geographical treatise, for he looked upon the Mount Everest expedition as too mundane to be given space in a spiritual book. (*The Statesman, Calcutta, January 1, 1931.*)

Of the first Everest expedition he merely wrote, "A party went up the mountain: although they stopped there twenty days, they failed to reach the summit and returned without causing trouble." The Lāma relates how some porters were killed on the last Mount Everest expedition, and how the chief Sahib sent a message with money asking for blessings upon the deceased: he writes "I performed the service with zeal, thinking in my mind how these souls had "suffered, and all for the sake of nothing."

Mr. Van Manen has summed up the difficulties of Tibetan geography as follows:—

"Geographical observation, local knowledge and a knowledge of the language have to "be brought together. Hitherto the three sources of information have remained apart. "The ritualistic Tibetan who reads mystical names in books cannot identify them with "geographical features. Not all Tibetans in one neighbourhood identify the peaks in the "same manner. The geographer may be misled by synonyms or by information from igno-"rant porters."

Sarat Chandra Das, who was always interested in geography, obtained from the authorities at Lhāsa a list of "the twenty most important mountains in all Tibet." His list was as follows :—

1. Thanlha.
2. Tise.
3. Man-mkhar.
4. Bule.
5. Star-sgo.
6. Plio-la.
7. Mkhahri.
8. Jomo kha-nag.
9. Rdo rye.
10. Gans-bzan.
11. Ptse-rdun.
12. La-phyi.
13. Tshe-rin.
14. Sna-nam.
15. Te-sgro.
16. Hod-se gan-rgyal.
17. Yar-lha cam-po.
18. Gsal-tje.
19. Ha-bo gans-bzan.
20. Tsa-ri na-lahi-gans.

These twenty names have some appearance of geographical reality, for the second name evidently denotes Kentaisse (Kailās) and the thirteenth name is Morshead's name for Gauri Sankar. The twelfth name is said by Sarat Chandra to belong to a mountain (Lapchyi) standing north of Everest—compare Howard Bury: *Mount Everest*, p. 326. Name No. 7 is probably Chomo Lhāri, and No. 1 may be Nyenchen-tang-lha.

The Devadhunga Controversy.

When in 1855 the Surveyor General, Sir Andrew Waugh, first suggested that the newly discovered highest peak should be named Mount Everest, Mr. Brian Hodgson, who had been Political Officer in Nepāl for many years, intimated to scientific societies that Waugh had been mistaken and that the mountain had a local name, Devadhunga. Hodgson was a scientist of high reputation; not only was he distinguished as an ethnologist and as a naturalist, but he had made profound studies of the different languages in vogue in Nepāl. In 1927 Sir George Grierson in the "Linguistic Survey of India" wrote, "The first attempts "at classifying the mass of Tibeto-Chinese languages were made by Brian "Hodgson, *clarum et venerabile nomen*, and his works still form the foundation "of all similar undertakings. Hodgson's classification holds good for the "entire field of Himālayan philology." The case of Brian Hodgson shows that a good linguist may be an unsound geographer. When Hodgson attempted to identify his mountain Devadhunga with Mount Everest, Colonel Waugh wrote as follows: "Mr. Hodgson endeavoured to establish the identity of Mount Everest "with Devadhunga. His arguments were so palpably conjectural, resting on "hearsay evidence alone, that I thought it needless to refute them as their "fallacious character was apparent to any person competent to understand the "subject. The true geographical latitude and longitude of Devadhunga are "unknown to Mr. Hodgson, or even its true bearing and distance from any "locality. Its height also is unknown. All these elements are necessary "for the identification of that mountain. The appearance of a mountain is an

"uncertain test, but even that test is wanting in Mr. Hodgson's case as he has
"never seen Devadhunga. The sketch map published by him gives his idea of
"that part of the Himālayas; a more erroneous impression was never formed.
"He represents a solitary mountain occupying a vast tract. This single
"mountain, however, is entirely imaginary."* Mr. Hodgson replied as follows:
"Colonel Waugh may be assured that his Mount Everest is far from lacking
"native names, and I will add that I should venture in any case of a natural
"object occurring in Nepāl to furnish the Colonel with its true native name,
"nay, several (for the country is very polyglottic), upon his furnishing me
"with the distance and bearings of that object, although neither I nor any
"European had gone near it."

This difference of opinion, of idea and of outlook between Waugh the surveyor and Hodgson the linguist, is of interest even now: the two men were irreconcilable.

Summing up the controversy from a geographical point of view, I have only to draw attention to the following facts:—in 1904 Captain H. Wood visited Nepāl, and observed the principal peaks and consulted all the Nepālese authorities on the subject, and he did not hear the name Devadhunga mentioned. In 1907 surveyor Natha Singh surveyed the Nepālese slopes of Mount Everest and he did not hear the name Devadhunga. General Bruce when in Nepāl did not hear it, nor did the Mount Everest expedition, nor did the recent Nepāl survey expedition.

The explanation of Hodgson's action probably is, that he had learnt the name Devadhunga from Nepālese literature and that he regarded it as a mystic name suitable for Mount Everest. We can, however, sympathise with the Surveyor General, scientific and precise in all his work, when he declined Hodgson's offer of any number of names for any mountain.

The Gauri Sankar Controversy.

In 1855 Hermann de Schlagintweit, a scientific observer of high repute, undertook a mission to India at the instance of the King of Prussia and with the concurrence of Lord Dalhousie. The new peak of Mount Everest had lately been discovered and Schlagintweit determined to observe it himself from two different directions, that is from Sikkim and from Nepāl. He was pursued by ill fortune: when he tried to observe Mount Everest from Sikkim, the peak of Makālu was standing in the way and this peak was so high and impressive that Schlagintweit mistook it for Everest. It was Makālu that he drew as Everest both in his panorama of the snows, and in his well-known landscape picture now preserved at the India Office.

When he moved to Nepāl and tried to observe Mount Everest from Kaulia, the most prominent peak in that direction was Gauri Sankar, and now for the

---

* Proc. R. G. S. Vol. I., p. 345; quoted by Sven Hedin in "Southern Tibet," Vol. III, 105.

second time he was misled. When drawing his panorama from Kaulia he overlooked the real Everest peak, and he wrote "Everest" against the Gauri Sankar peak. As a geographer Schlagintweit was superior to Hodgson: he was an accurate observer and draftsman. From his drawings General Walker, who had succeeded Waugh as Surveyor General in India, was able to prove by trigonometrical calculations that Mount Everest had not been shown in Schlagintweit's panorama and that the peak which he marked "Everest" was the Survey peak XX, height 23,440 feet. It had not been possible for the Survey to combat the vagueness of Hodgson by means of calculations, but Schlagintweit's panoramas were so accurate that the Survey was able to superimpose their own observations upon his drawings, and they thus discovered his error in the identification of Mount Everest.

Indian geography owes much to Hermann de Schlagintweit, and it has been a misfortune that his errors should have had unceasing attention from controversies, and that his more valuable contributions should have been silently absorbed and forgotten.

Schlagintweit was a Himālayan pioneer, and in his time mountaineers had not realised that the Himālayan problems were different from those of the Alps. They had not realised the immensity of the Himālayan area, nor the countless ranges of innumerable peaks obscuring one another. If Mount Everest had been standing on the Alps, it would have been visible from Switzerland and Italy. And when Schlagintweit saw Makālu standing in the direction of Everest and surpassing all its neighbours in height, he assumed without doubt that it must be Everest, and his assumption was not unreasonable. Schlagintweit's assumption was wrong, but it taught a useful lesson and it brought home to observers how easy it is to mistake one peak for another when they are confronted by a whole sea of peaks.

Mr. Freshfield continued the Gauri Sankar controversy after General Walker had settled the questions in dispute. In March 1903, he wrote in the "Geographical Journal" as follows:— "The reason for which the surveyors argued so "strenuously forty-five years ago that the 29,002 ft. peak could not 'be the Gauri Sankar of Nepāl was, of course, that their chief's proceeding in "giving the mountain an English name was excused or justified at the time by "the assertion that it had no local or native name." The surveyors whose motives Mr. Freshfield impugned were formed into a committee in 1859 to consider the question of the identity of two peaks. From geographical evidence available, they concluded that the two peaks were not identical, and their conclusion has been found correct.

In 1903 Captain Wood visited Kaulia by order of Lord Curzon. He found that Mount Everest and Gauri Sankar were different peaks thirty-six miles apart, and that the imposing peak of the snowy range, known to the Survey as peak XX, was the famous Gauri Sankar of the Nepālese. He also discovered that Everest, far from being conspicuous, was almost obscured from view by intervening ranges.

Chomo Lungma.

In his book "Twenty years in the Himālaya" published in 1910, General Bruce wrote that he had heard the name Chomo Lungma applied to Mount Everest by Bhotiās in Nepāl, but he did not press for its adoption. It was not heard again by European geographers until 1921, when the expedition under Colonel Howard Bury made the first attempt to climb Mount Everest. In the official passport given to Howard Bury, the name mentioned was Chama-Lung, which has a different meaning from Chomo Lungma. In 1926 Sir Sven Hedin published at Leipzig a book on Mount Everest, in which he pointed out that the Lāmas who made their survey of Tibet in 1711 had entered the name Tchoumou Lancma on their map of the Mount Everest region. The problem of this Tibetan name was considered in a Professional Paper of the Survey of India, published as No. 26 of 1931, and the conclusion was reached that some such name as Chomo Lungma is in use by local Bhotiās and applied to a mountain region.

When the Survey were observing the Nepāl peaks from the plains of India in 1849-1855, they designated Mount Everest by the symbol XV; the peaks which they designated XIV and XVI were lower peaks standing twenty miles south of Mount Everest, and both these peaks XIV and XVI were named Tschamlang by the Survey.*

The prefix Chomo is very common in North-eastern Nepāl and the adjoining part of Tibet: we find Chomo Lhari, Chomo Kankar, Chomo Uri, Chomo Tsering. The word Lungma without Chomo is also one of the commonest names in Tibet. In some of the survey maps of Western Tibet the name Lungma occurs forty or fifty times in a single sheet. (See Atlas quarter sheets, 45 N. W. and 45 N. E.). It is also attached to glaciers like the Chogo Lungma, and to passes like the Lungma La, twenty miles east of Mount Everest, and the Lungma La between Abor and Tibet (*Record Vol. IV, 1914, p. 66*). When the new survey sheets of Ladākh and Baltistān were being compiled, it was decided to drop the word Lungma as being too frequently used in Colonel Montgomerie's atlas sheets and as being more probably a noun than a name. The best service which explorers will be able to do in future is to teach the Tibetans to adopt the name Mount Everest.

The Kānchenjunga Controversies.

Kānchenjunga is the mountain of Sikkim, and Sikkim is the name given to the Himālayan area which is drained by the river Tīsta. The population of central Sikkim forms part of the Tibeto-Burman race, and they speak a language

---

* The higher of the two appeared as Chamlang in Table V of the first edition of this paper, 1907: it appears as peak Chamlang in Table V of the present edition.

known as Lepcha; the Linguistic Survey gives 35,000 as the number of Lepcha speakers. The northern portion of Sikkim is peopled by a section of the Tibetan race, the Sikkim Bhotiās, and they speak a dialect of Tibetan known as Da-njong-ka (20,000 speakers). In the lower hills and terai the Bengalis predominate, whilst the population of the Darjeeling district is largely Nepālese. The following names are given to the mountain of Sikkim:—

People.	Name.	Authority.
Lepchas	Kong Lo Chu	Waddell.
Nepāl Bhotiās	Kang-chen	Hodgson.
Sikkim Bhotiās	Khambu-Karma	Sandberg.
Nepālese tribes	Khumbh-Karan Langur	Hodgson.
Tibetans of Sikkim	Gans-chhen-mdzod-lnga *	Van Manen.
Indians	Kānchenjunga	Imperial Gazetteer and Surveyor General.

It may be thought that the people of Sikkim should be allowed to name the mountains of their country, and that other races should accept their decisions. This rule holds good in the case of local objects such as minor peaks, valleys and towns, but when a mountain is so high as to be visible for over one hundred miles beyond the Sikkim borders, the trans-border populations will have their own names for it also. For centuries the people dwelling in the hot plains of Bengal have been observing with wonder this peak of snow on their northern horizon. The inhabitants of Tibet may have been observing the same peak, but not with the same admiration, as their country is cold, and they have snow peaks on all their horizons.

Along the ethnographic frontier of India we find certain mountains that have both Sanskrit and Tibetan names:

Kailās (Tibetan, Kangrimpoche).
Gurla Mandhāta (Tibetan, Memo-nam-nyim-ri).
Gosainthān (Tibetan, Shisha Pungma).
Gauri Sankar (Tibetan, Trashi-Tsering).

These ancient Sanskrit names were given by Hindu pilgrims to snow mountains situated near shrines of sanctity, and in a later era the same mountains have become goals of Buddhist pilgrimage and have received Tibetan names.

Kānchenjunga, the mountain of Sikkim, is the only instance of the same name, or almost the same name, being adopted by both the Indian and Tibetan peoples.

---

* The written form of the Tibetan name; the colloquial equivalent is Kang-chhen-dzo-nga.

There has been a controversy over the Sanskrit and Tibetan names—as to which of them originated first. It is possible that both the Sanskrit and Tibetan names have been evolved side by side, not in conflict but in mutual help; it is possible that both forms have now become deserving of preservation through their separate growths, for growth and evolution are more important than origin. Tibetan linguists have rejected the Sanskrit origin of the name, but the supposed Tibetan origin itself is not free from uncertainty.

The following is a brief outline of the history of the geographical name Kānchenjunga :—

1711.—Chinese Lāmas made a map of Tibet, upon which they showed the mountain Chomo Lhāri; they also showed the high mountain of Sikkim, but gave it the name of Rimo-la.

1828-1836.—Klaproth published Chinese maps of Tibet, which have been eulogised by Markham and Sven Hedin. Klaproth showed the Sikkim mountain but gave to it the name Djimoula. His maps corrected the mistakes of the Lāmas in the positions of the mountain and of the town of Phari. (For Klaproth's maps see Sven Hedin's *Southern Tibet*, Volumes I, II and VII.)

1847.—The Survey of India fixed the great Sikkim mountain by observations taken from the plains of Bengal and the outer hills. The Survey officers were British with Bengali assistants. They gave the name Kangchanjunga (so spelt) to the mountain. This was the first appearance in geography of the now famous name and *it came from the side of India.* The Tibetan surveys of the Sikkim mountain were made 135 years before the Indian surveys, but the fact is clear in history that the name came from India and not from Tibet.

Professor Suniti Kumar Chatterji writes that though the Bengali surveyors may have been mistaken, yet they were firm believers in the Sanskrit name when they gave it to the Survey in 1847. Their view was accepted also by Bengali writers, and there are thus over eighty years of usage in Bengali for the Sanskritised form. From Bengali the Sanskrit form has spread to Hindi and other Indian languages.

The professor was writing of the historic period since 1847; but when I see the interest taken in the Himālayan snow-peaks of Nanda Devi and Dhaulāgiri by dwellers in the plains of India, it seems inconceivable that the inhabitants of northern Bengal should have had no name, during the pre-historic centuries, for the peak of perpetual snow which was presenting such a strange contrast to their own hot climate.

1854.—Sir Joseph Hooker brought the name to the notice of the European public in his "Himālayan Journals." Although in his map he used the name

Kangchenjunga in keeping with Waugh's survey map, yet throughout his book he spelt it as Kinchinjunga. He was therefore responsible for the first divergence in spelling.

1857.—Brian Hodgson, the Nepāl linguist, drew his map of the Himālayas and showed the high mountain of Sikkim as Kangchen but without the termination "junga."

1867.—The Survey published a map upon which the name was spelt Kantschin-dschinga. From 1847 to 1867 no spelling had been laid down by authority and every map-maker followed his own ideas.

1872.—The Hunterian system of transliteration was accepted by the Government of India. The right of individual opinion was taken away, and a system of uniformity was introduced. The Imperial Gazetteer was to be issued as the authority and arbitrator.

1881.—When the Gazetteer was first issued the Sanskrit spelling Kanchanjanga was introduced by Sir William Hunter. Unfortunately Hooker's journals were more widely known than the Imperial Gazetteer, and Hunter's decision was not generally accepted. The 11th edition Encyclopædia Britannica gave Hooker's anglicised form Kinchinjunga as preferable, and Hunter's form Kanchanjanga as alternative. In subsequent editions of the Encyclopædia the form Kinchinjunga alone has been given. Constable in 1893 adopted Hunter's Sanskrit form.

Fullarton's Gazetteer and Lippincott's Gazetteer, 1906, adhered to Hooker's form Kinchinjunga.

1882.—Although Hodgson had heard Tibetans use the name Kangchen it does not appear that the full Tibetan name Gans-chhen-mdzod-lnga (or Kangchhen-dzo-nga) ever came into geography through surveyors or explorers learning it from Tibetans in the field. It seems to have been a theoretical name introduced in 1881 by Dr. Jeaschke when he was compiling his Tibetan dictionary. It was introduced to give a Tibetan explanation of the Indian termination "junga." Dr. Jeaschke's theoretical name has had wide influence during the last fifty years, its form and spelling have been accepted at Lhāsa, and are spreading through Tibet. There is no objection to his version being accepted for Tibetan maps. The Bengalis may possibly have built their name Kanchenjunga upon the Tibetan foundation Kangchhen, but the Tibetans may also have derived their termination mdzod-lnga from the Bengali termination "junga."

1900.—When the Secretary of State gave his assent to the Hunterian system, he suggested in his despatch that "some extension should be given to that "part of the scheme which permits a departure from the new system in the case "of those places of which the names have acquired a widely recognised mode of "spelling, either from popular custom or in consequence of historical notoriety."

At the beginning of the present century, when the new edition of the Imperial Gazetteer was being prepared, Kanchenjunga was included amongst the names falling under the Secretary of State's despatch, and two forms of spelling now became permissible. The primary form was Hooker's anglicised Kinchinjunga, and the alternative spelling was the Indianised form Kanchenjunga. The official arbitration thus allowed two different spellings, and this step has given rise to the idea that the question of spelling has not been finally decided.

1903.—In 1903 the Survey of India issued a new map of Sikkim, which was compiled from data supplied by the Quartermaster General; and on this map they spelt the mountain name as Kangchenjunga. This departure on the part of the Survey from the Imperial Gazetteer was probably due to the divided responsibility for this map. The Sikkim map was issued when Colonel Gore was Surveyor General. Colonel Gore was always firm in his support of co-operation and uniformity, and I am convinced that he never authorised the spelling Kangchenjunga.

1904.—Sir Thomas Holdich adopted Kanchanjanga in his book "India" and Mr. Freshfield published his book on "Kangchenjunga." The latter adopted the spelling employed in Colonel Gore's 1903 map. Mr. Freshfield was thus justified in his action. Other mountaineering authors have followed Mr. Freshfield in using the spelling Kangchenjunga. But it is a spelling that does not meet with general approval, for it combines the Tibetan sound Kang with the purely Indian termination "junga." In 1910 General Bruce adopted "Kinchenjanga," an Indianised form.

1931.—The Surveyor General (Brigadier Thomas) has recently made a new appeal for uniformity by abandoning Hooker's form of spelling and by introducing the Indianised form Kānchenjunga into the Survey. It is to be hoped that his action will meet with co-operation.

The spelling "Kānchenjunga" is not an exact reproduction of the Sanskrit form Kanchanjhanga, but no objection can be raised on this account, for the modern Hindu spellings of Gauri Sankar, Dhaulāgiri, Gosainthān, and Kedārnāth are not exact reproductions of the ancient Sanskrit. But the spelling "Kānchanjunga" would have been equally suitable.

The form Kānchenjunga is one of the two forms that have always been permitted by the later edition of the Imperial Gazetteer, and it differs in only one letter from the spelling adopted by Sir William Hunter in the first edition. It is not a Tibeto-Indian compromise.

The spelling Kānchenjunga was moreover adopted as the correct Indianised form by the two most prominent Indian authorities on Tibetan names, Colonel Waddell and Sarat Chandra Das, C.I.E. In his Tibetan dictionary, 1902, Sarat Chandra Das accepted the form Kānchenjunga.

In recent years the Times newspaper in its accounts of Kānchenjunga expeditions has supported the authority of the Imperial Gazetteer and has adhered to the form Kanchenjunga.

The Tibetan Name for Kānchenjunga.

The question of the Tibetan name for Kānchenjunga is surrounded with difficulties. Geographers are dependent upon the advice of linguists, and whilst they have sincere admiration for the knowledge of the latter, they are at times disquieted to find that the linguistic aims and ideas differ from their own. Waugh discovered this in his discussions with Brian Hodgson (see page 23, Chapter 3).

The fact that the written Tibetan name differs materially from the colloquial name is a source of geographical trouble. The written Tibetan name for Sikkim is Hbras-Yongs, the colloquial Tibetan name is Denjong (Bell). The chief authority on the Tibetan language in India is Mr. Van Manen: and when Herr Bauer the leader of the 1929 expedition asked Mr. Van Manen's advice, the latter replied that the correct Tibetan spelling for Kānchenjunga is Gans-chhen-mdzod-lnga, but that as Herr Bauer was writing a book of travel and not a scientific treatise, he might adopt the colloquial spelling Kang-chhen-dzo-nga.* (*Bauer: Im Kampf um den Himalaja.*)

The name Gans-chhen-mdzod-lnga seems to have originated from the difficulty that linguists had in finding a Tibetan equivalent for the Indian termination "junga." The Tibetan name Kang-chhen had been undoubtedly derived from the Sikkimese. The three letters nga in Tibetan mean five, but even then it was difficult to explain "junga." So Dr. Jeaschke introduced mdzod-lnga in place of junga, and mdzod-lnga means "five repositories." The whole Tibetan name Gans-chhen-mdzod-lnga thus meant "the five repositories of great snow."

In the learned note that Mr. Van Manen wrote for Herr Bauer, he explained that when Dr. Jeaschke introduced into his dictionary of 1881 his now well-known Tibetan spelling "Gans-chhen-mdzod-lnga, the five receptacles of the vast glacier ice," he added also an alternative version "Gans-chhen-rje-lnga,

---

* Maps are scientific documents used in international agreements: the correct form of spelling in preference to the colloquial is invariably adopted on the maps of the Ordnance Survey of Great Britain.

meaning the five kings of the vast glacier ice." To a linguistic enthusiast seeking for an explanation of the Indian "junga" the introduction of two different versions may seem natural and scientific, but to the geographer, who wants to know what the people themselves say, the introduction of two different explanations seems to detract from the value of both.

The different versions suggested by linguists for the Tibetan name of Kānchenjunga may be summed up as follows:—

Name.	Meaning.	Authority.
Gans-chhen-mdzod-lnga	Five receptacles of vast glacier ice.	Jeaschke, 1881.
Gans-chhen-rje-lnga	Five kings of vast ice	Jeaschke, 1881.
Gans-chhen-rtse-lnga	Five great glacier peaks	....
Kang-chhen-dzo-nga	Five repositories of great snows.	Waddell, 1891.
Kang-chhen-dso-nga	Five treasure chests of great snow.	Sandberg, 1895.
Gans-chhen-mced-lnga	Five brethren of great snows	Ribbach, 1929.
Gans-chhen-mdzod-lnga	Five receptacles of vast glacier ice.	Van Manen, 1931.
Kanchen-junga, (Indianised, from the Sanskrit).	Golden thigh	Imperial Gazetteer.

It will be seen from this table that the termination has been a source of trouble to Tibetan linguists. No Tibetan substitute for the Indian "junga" has been agreed upon. The variety of the attempts to find a substitute is an indication of uncertainty.

Colonel Waddell has explained that "the five repositories of great snow," mean the five peaks of Kānchenjunga; other writers have said that they mean the five glaciers. But the word "five" seems out of place applied to Kānchenjunga. As applied to Gauri Sankar it had a meaning, for Morshead found five similar sister peaks standing in juxta position. But Kānchenjunga is an immense pyramid, and only one side of it can be viewed at a time. The Lepchas have truly named it "the high screen of snows," for it screens everything behind it. The geographer has a right to ask, why should Kānchenjunga be called "five peaks" or "five glaciers;" six peaks or ten or fifty would be equally applicable. The word five has no explanation in the topography. It has been said that when we view Kānchenjunga from Darjeeling, we see five prominent peaks. But the Tibetans dwell to the north-east of the mountain, and Darjeeling is situated to the south-west. Why should Tibetans invent a name to suit a foreign aspect of the mountain? Darjeeling is now a popular hill-station, but a hundred years ago it was only a Lepcha town. Its name is Lepcha.

If we consider the peaks that stand in the vicinity of Kānchenjunga, Jonsong is a Tibetan name, but Kabru and Jano are names not used by Tibetans (Bell). Pandim is a Lepcha name, and Narsing is an Indian names. In Chapter 22 which describes the Tīsta river a note has been included, in which it is shown that the Private Secretary to the Maharajah of Sikkim does not agree with the view that the name Kānchenjunga has been derived from five peaks or five glaciers or five treasuries of snow.

I feel sure that linguists will realize the uncertainty that has been experienced by surveyors who have had to decide upon one definite form of spelling. Linguists have looked upon the name Kang-chhen-dzo-nga as though it were a Lhāsa Tibetan name, but it was a Da-njong-ka name used only in Sikkim. Whether this name is of ancient or recent standing in Sikkim cannot be discovered, but that it has only recently been recognised in Lhāsa seems certain. In Sikkim the Tibetans constitute a small minority of the population.

The following letter from Sir Charles Bell, who was the political officer in Sikkim, illustrates the difficulties with which surveyors were confronted when they were conversing with the hill people. "The Sikkimese," he writes, "do "not as a rule use the whole word Kang-chhen-dzo-nga, but more often simply "Kang-chhen. A great many apply the name Kang-chhen to the other mountain "Kabru, because throughout a great part of Sikkim Kabru is the more cons-"picuous mountain of the two. Kang-chhen is not a well-known Tibetan moun-"tain; for every Tibetan who knows Kang-chhen five hundred will know Chomo "Lhāri."

The original meaning of the Sanskrit name was "the mountain of the golden thigh," the word golden having reference to the effects of sunrise and sunset upon the mountain. Geographers see with surprise that Colonel Waddell, the linguistic authority, became annoyed with the Tibetans of Sikkim when he found them accepting the Indian idea in preference to his "five repositories of great snow." In his book "Among the Himālayas," 1900, p. 386, he writes, "Kānchenjunga is called by Tibetans the repository of gold. This name it "seems to me has arisen from the interpretation of the popular name in too "literal and mythological a manner. The name Kānchenjunga is Tibetan and "means literally the five repositories of the great glaciers and it is physically "descriptive of its five peaks."

It is possible that these Tibetans obtained their ideas of gold from the Indian name "golden thigh." The Sikkim manual of worship for the mountain god speaks of a treasury of gold, the lofty peak being gilded by the rising and setting sun.

For maps of Tibet the name regarded as authoritative by Van Manen in 1931, namely Gans-chhen-mdzod-lnga, should I think be accepted: but for maps of India Kānchenjunga should be retained.

Even if the Indian and Tibetan names have emanated from one origin, they have followed different courses of evolution. Hitherto we have been trying to force the two names by compromises into one spelling. It will be better in future to recognise that the two names have diverged so widely in their growth that they cannot now be both represented by one and the same formula. In accepting two forms of spelling we shall be recognising them as two different names and shall be treating them as we treat the Indian and Tibetan names for Kailās and Gauri Sankar.

The Sanskrit Name Kancan-jangha.

A surveyor has to learn the pronunciation of geographical names from the people and to convert them into written words. An etymologist is interested in discovering the ancient origins of names. Prudent surveyors refrain from trespassing upon the etymologists' ground. In 1835 the explorer Vigne ventured to explain the origins of certain names in Kashmīr, and he has been held up as a warning to trespassers. His case is quoted by Sir Aurel Stein as showing that a geographer may be a bad etymologist. (*Ancient Geography of Kashmīr.*) The Sanskrit origin of the name Kānchenjunga has been explained by Mahamahopadhyaya Dr. Hara Prasad Shastri as having been "Kancan-jangha," the golden thigh. The spelling of the name, he says, according to the Geneva Convention adopted by all Sanskritists throughout the world, is Kancana-jangha, (for ordinary purposes Kancan-jangha).*

The objection has been raised that the shape of the mountain bears no resemblance to an inverted thigh, that the mountain has a pointed summit whereas a thigh (cut off at the knee) does not terminate in a point. From Purnea in Bihār, however, Kānchenjunga has the appearance of being a high point on a jagged ridge; the following passage is quoted from Colonel Tanner's report, 1883—"Kabru (24,002 feet) is connected with the second peak of Kān-"chenjunga (27,803 feet) by a ridge, the lowest depression of which has an alti-"tude of 22,100 feet".

The Sanskrit name Kancan-jangha may have been given to the mountain by pandits in comparatively recent times, like the name Nanga Parbat in Kashmīr. No etymologist has claimed that the Sanskrit name Kancan-jangha is of great antiquity.

A further note on the name Kānchenjunga has been added in Appendix 3 of Part III of this book, in reply to certain criticisms of the name, that have been published in the Himālayan Journal of 1932.

*Himālayan Journal, III, p. 154.

The Karakorum Controversy.

The length of the Karakorum range has been proved by Sven Hedin to be so great, that it will be found advisable for geographical purposes to subdivide it into sections, as has already been done in the cases of the Alps, the Rockies, the Andes, and the Himālayas. In all these ranges the mountain names have been preserved throughout their lengths, and the sectional names have been taken from the countries which the ranges traverse or border. The Andes have been subdivided into the Chilian Andes, the Peruvian Andes, and the Patagonian; the great Himālayan range has been subdivided into the Punjab Himālayas, the Kumaun Himālayas, the Nepāl and the Assam. The Punjab Himālayas are the Himālayas seen from the Punjab and drained by the Punjab rivers: they contain the "Punjab Hill States". The Hindu Kush are divided into the Afghān Hindu Kush and the Chitrāl Hindu Kush. If we adhere to this world-wide precedent and to this approved geographical method,—and I do not think that we can improve on it,—we shall subdivide the Karakorum into—

(1) the Hunza Karakorum,
(2) the Balti Karakorum,
(3) the Depsang Karakorum, and
(4) the Tibetan Karakorum.

The question whether the Karakorum range should be regarded as one great range or as two parallel ranges does not affect the fundamental nomenclature; if we look at such a problem from a synthetic point of view, we can hardly avoid the conclusion that the main Karakorum crest, the Masherbrum ridge, and the watershed range are component parts of one orographical whole. But if the details are examined from an analytical point of view, it may be found convenient to distinguish the separate parts by different names. It is always advisable to begin with synthesis and to limit the analytic process as much as possible. The question of analysis will be considered in the second part of this book.

A controversy has however at times arisen over the *name* "Karakorum," and in this chapter the question is being considered whether the name Karakorum could with advantage be replaced by Muztāgh (or by Muztāgh-Karakorum, *vide* Geogr. Journ., April 1927, p. 327; also Sept. 1929 and August 1930). All along the frontiers of India the names of passes are well known, and the names of passes, as I have already pointed out in this chapter, come to be transferred to the mountain ranges. The two passes over the Karakorum range have been known for centuries as the Muztāgh and the Karakorum, and it has been only natural, as was pointed out by Drew in 1875, that both these names should have come to be applied by travellers to different parts of the same range, the name Muztāgh on the west of Baltistān and the name Karakorum on the east. Both these pass-names are foreign names, but as I have also shown in this chapter, the pass-names over our trans-frontier ranges generally do spring from the foreign languages spoken beyond them. And thus it has come about that although the mountain names of Baltistān, such as Gasherbrum, Baltoro, Chogo Lungma, Rimo are all Tibetan, the two pass-names are both Turki. I see no objection to this: the Tibetan pass-names Zoji La and Lipu Lekh and the Afghān pass-name Khaibar are quite well known to Indians, and the Turki pass-names Muztāgh and Karakorum are known to Balti Tibetans.*

When scientific maps are being prepared, geographers find it inconvenient to have two names applied to the same mountain range within a relatively short distance of one another. Our predecessors found it unnecessary to describe the range as the "Muztāgh or Karakorum," and so the responsible authorities, Sir Clements Markham in London in 1871 and General Walker in India in 1876, decided to drop the name Muztāgh and to apply the name Karakorum to the whole range. William Moorcroft in 1820 was the first European explorer to introduce the name "Karakorum mountains." In 1831 Grimm's map snowed "Karakorum Gebirge" along the northern bank of the Indus. In 1830 and 1844 Humboldt gave the name Karakorum to the central range of the Tibet plateau, and Humboldt's authority has been recognised by the geographers of Europe (*Sven Hedin: Southern Tibet, VII, XXXII*). Humboldt applied the name Muztāgh to the Tien Shan range, on the authority of the Emperor Bābar's memoirs. In 1854 Alexander Cunningham and Henry Strachey made surveys of Western Tibet: Cunningham wrote that he found Moorcroft absolutely trustworthy and one of the most conscientious men that ever lived. Strachey wrote that he owed almost all his nomenclature to Moorcroft. In a recent paper Sir Aurel Stein has lamented that no biography has been written of so great a geographer as Moorcroft (*Life of Theodore Duka, 1914*). The story that Moorcroft travelled to Lhāsa had no foundation: he sacrificed his life in his enthusiasm for geographical exploration, and he was at Andkhui, north of the Hindu Kush when he died.

In 1855-1865 Colonel Montgomerie made his survey of Western Tibet and determined the heights and positions of the Karakorum peaks: he gave to his peaks the symbol K after the name Karakorum. In his reports he sometimes referred to the Karakorum range and sometimes to "the great range which is "called both Muztāgh and Karakorum". His assistant was Captain Godwin-Austen, who wrote two papers on the glaciers of the Muztāgh range: the glaciers which Godwin-Austen described were those near the Muztāgh section of the range and there was no significance in his reference to the Muztāgh range. On his grave near Guildford are engraved the words, "He surveyed the Kara-

---

*The Turki speaking people of Kāshgar are Mongolians and are closely related to the Baltis. The latter are the only Tibetans who have forsaken Buddhism and become Muhammadans: their conversion was probably due to the influence of Mongolian Muhammadans from Kāshgar.

"korum Range." The name Karakorum Range was definitely adopted for the maps of the Government of India in 1876.*

In 1907 I referred the question of the name to Colonel Wauhope, who was an oriental scholar, and who had passed his career in the mountains of the northwest frontier, and who had only recently been surveying the Pāmirs and Hindu Kush: he wrote in reply—"Muztāghs are as common all over Central Asia as "Safed Kohs on our north-west frontier. The name Karakorum is quite "established now for the mountain range separating the Indus and Zarafshān, and "is the most suitable."

If the name Karakorum was considered more suitable than Muztāgh in 1876, its superiority has been enhanced during the last fifty years by the modern application of the name Muztāgh to other high mountains. It has been said that the name Karakorum is as common in Turkistān as the name Muztāgh. In Stein's list of the geographical names of Chinese Turkistān the name Karakorum only appears twice outside the Karakorum range, and on neither of these occasions is its use of any geographical significance. (*Memoir by Sir Aurel Stein; Record Volume XVII, Survey of India.*) If we take a generalised fundamental map like Stein's map of Chinese Turkistān, published by the Royal Geographical Society (*scale $\frac{1}{5M}$, Geographical Journal, May 1925*), we see that beyond the Karakorum range there are only three mountain names of sufficient importance to be entered on such a map, and they are—

(1) Muztāgh Ata peak, (on the Muztāgh Ata range),
(2) Kungur,
(3) Muztāgh peak, (on the Kunlun range).

Two out of these three primary mountain names are Muztāgh; and there is also the Muztāgh Ata range; if we had three high mountains in Europe all named Mont Blanc, the confusion would become intolerable. We ought therefore to avoid any further extension of the name Muztāgh as a primary mountain name in Asia; and we ought to adhere loyally to the decision of Moorcroft, Markham and Walker, and to uphold the fine distinctive name of Karakorum.

The Karakorum Pass.

The Karakorum Pass is famous in both the history and the geography of Asia. It has been said that this pass is not on the Karakorum range. It is not on the crest-line of the range, but it is a pass over the range. A range is not a single line, it is a massive fold of rock, one hundred miles wide, that has been raised up out of the earth's crust. The fact that the Shyok river has cut its way back through the southern flank of this range and through its crest-line to the

---

* In 1862 the Schlagintweit brothers adopted the name "Karakorum Range," *vide* Sven Hedin's *Southern Tibet*, III, 169. In 1875 Stieler adopted Karakorum, and gave the name Muztāgh to the Kāshgar range. Subsequently Sven Hedin applied the name Muztāgh to this Kāshgar range, and Sir Aurel Stein has called it the Muztāgh Ata range. The application of the name Muztāgh to this Kāshgar range renders the name Muztāgh undesirable and unsuitable for the Karakorum range.

Karakorum pass is a phenomenon that has many parallels in Asia. In their book on the Karakorum glaciers, Dr. and Mrs. Visser show how the Hunza and Gilgit rivers have cut back through the Karakorum crest; what has occurred in Hunza has occurred also in Depsang. The Karakorum range, the Karakorum watershed and the Karakorum pass form a scientific triad of names, and their triple accordance impresses upon us the lesson that the range, the watershed and the pass are parts of one geographical whole. (This question will be considered in greater detail in Chapter 14 of Part II.)

The meaning and history of the name Karakorum.

The word Kara means black, and Korum means fallen rock or gravel. It has been suggested that it is not suitable to apply a name meaning black to a snow-mountain. Muztāgh means snow-mountain, but this name has already been used too frequently to be any longer distinctive. The name Kara-Kul, black lake, is said by Hedin and Wauhope to have originated from the sudden storms which break over it. Dr. Visser has written that he sees no objection to a name meaning black being used for a snow-mountain, and I do not think that the original meaning of a word as used in conversation should be literally considered, when it has been compounded with other words into a geographical name. There is a Himālayan river named the Kāli Ganga (Black river) and another the Dhauli Ganga (White river): both these rivers have dark depths and both have cataracts of white foam; their two names are in artistic contrast and are scientifically distinctive, and it would be wrong to test them by literalism.

Colonel Wood has been a strong supporter of the old name Karakorum. Referring to the Karakorum pass in 1922, he raised an interesting question, but without any desire to introduce a change. He wrote,—

"It is difficult to understand why this pass received the name Karakorum, which means "black rock: the formation is red sandstone and the most noticeable colour is yellow".

If therefore the name Karakorum is unsuitable for a white mountain, it is equally unsuitable for a yellow and red pass. Yet it would be indeed ridiculous to change the name of this historic pass, a name known for centuries to the peoples of Asia. Colonel Wood's note led me to study the history of this pass and of its name. Dr. Arthur Neve wrote (*Thirty Years in Kashmīr, 1913*: quoted by Sven Hedin in *Southern Tibet*), "The trade route over the Kara-"korum pass has been used from time immemorial. Rock inscriptions show "that it was used centuries before the Christian era. Chinese armies have "swept over it, and for centuries the Chinese held fortified posts along it. Indian "conquerors have defied climatic difficulties, and have established colonies on "the north side in the basin of the Tārīm".

In the 13th Century, Gengkis Khan the Mongol, who ranks as a military leader with Caesar and Napoleon, conquered the greater part of Asia and the south-eastern part of Europe: his empire extended from Pekin to Warsaw. If we go through Central Asia to-day, we are told that three men have conquered the world,—Alexander, Gengkis Khan and Tīmūr (*Lamb's History of Tamerlane*). Gengkis Khan founded the Mongol empire, and his capital city (now in ruins) was Karakorum in Mongolia. From the city of Karakorum Asia was governed, and the name Karakorum was known everywhere. The Imperial road from Delhi to Karakorum passed through Kashmir and Ladākh, and crossed over the pass now known to us as the Karakorum. In England we speak of the "London road," and the "Bath road;" in India we talk of the "Agra road" and the "Lahore road." At Delhi itself we have the "Kashmir Gate." In Ladākh to-day they say the "Leh road." Is it not likely that in the days of Gengkis Khan the people spoke of the "Karakorum road?" And their "Karakorum road" from India crossed the pass which to-day we call Karakorum. The culminating point of the long road from Delhi to Karakorum was the point we now name "Karakorum pass." I venture to submit that history has furnished the explanation of our geographical name Karakorum, which could not be learnt from the colour of the rocks.

When Dr. Neve wrote the passage which I have just quoted from him concerning the "Chinese" armies sweeping over the pass, and the "Chinese" fortified posts, I think that he must have been referring to the Mongols. Kublai Khan, the grandson of Gengkis Khan, moved the Mongol capital to Pekin and ruled over Tibet.

Alexander the Great was accompanied on his campaigns by historians: Julius Caesar was his own historian. The mausoleum and mosques of Tīmūr are still reverenced at Samarkand: the letters of Napoleon are preserved in the libraries of Europe. But no memorial of Gengkis Khan is to be seen in Asia.

The name of Gengkis Khan's capital Karakorum has, however, during the progress of geography in Western Tibet, come to be bestowed in the 19th century upon the highest mountains of his Empire. And it *is* in this way that geography has provided the memorial which archæology had failed to do.

The recent introduction of double names.

In 1927 a proposal was made to substitute new double names in place of the old simple names, that had become so well known. The following table gives the old names and the new proposals:—

	Existing names.	Double names proposed.
The Main Range	Karakorum	Muztāgh-Karakorum.
The Mountain Region	Karakorum	Karakorum-Himālaya.
Outer subsidiary range	Aghil	Aghil-Karakorum.
Inner subsidiary range	Kailās	Kailās-Karakorum.

At the meeting of the Royal Geographical Society in 1926 when these double names were first proposed, Colonel H. Wood made a protest against them, and he voiced the opinion of Survey officers, political officers, and sportsmen. The double name Karakorum-Himālaya was withdrawn at the advice of Dr. Longstaff, and surveyors felt indebted to him for his generous co-operation (*Geographical Journal, August 1930*).

The double names Kailās-Karakorum and Muztāgh-Karakorum are however being used. Attempts have been made to find precedents for them in the Alps, but there are no precedents there or elsewhere. In the Geographical Journal for August 1930 (p. 142) it was stated that the double name Kailās-Karakorum "is equivalent to the name Bernese Alps." The Bernese Alps are a subdivision of the Alpine Range: the name Bernese merely denotes that the subdivision is on the side of Berne. Kailās is the name given to a mountain range in south-western Tibet, *and Karakorum is the name given to a different mountain range in another province of Tibet*. The name Bernese Alps is a sectional and regional name, and is not the name of a long mountain chain. The name Kailās-Karakorum is not sectional and not regional: it is being proposed for a whole mountain range as long as the Alps. If we want a Balti parallel to the Bernese Alps, it must be Skārdu-Karakorum, for Skārdu is the capital of Baltistān, as Berne is of Switzerland. The name Kailās-Karakorum is a combination of names that geographers should avoid. Kailās is a Sanskrit name that came into Tibet from the south 30 centuries ago, the name Karakorum came into Tibet from the north 7 centuries ago. Both the Sanskrit and Mongolian names have an historic right to their own places in Tibet: but these places are 400 miles apart, and though the Kailās range is being found to approach the Karakorum, it is unwise to combine their names. In the vicissitudes of history anomalies may gain places in geography, but with care no confusion need arise. The double name will carry the name Karakorum into the region of the Mānasarowar lakes, and it will be out of place there.

In the Geographical Journal for August 1930, page 147, the name Muztāgh-Karakorum has again been compared with the names Bernese Alps and Punjab Himālaya. Neither of these comparisons holds good: Muztāgh-Karakorum is the name proposed for a great range that has always been known as Karakorum and that requires no second name; the names Bernese Alps and Punjab Himālaya are applicable to subdivisions only: the meanings of these two latter names are self-explanatory; but the combination Muztāgh-Karakorum has no meaning. (The question which has been raised as to the true *alignment* of the Karakorum range will be considered in Chapter 14 of Part II.)

CHAPTER 4.

NOTES ON CERTAIN IMPORTANT MOUNTAIN NAMES.

(a) Himālaya.

(b) Southern Tibet.

(c) Baltistān.

(d) Dardistān.

Himālaya, if not the oldest, is one of the oldest names in geography. The word is Sanskrit and means the abode of snow. During the Greek Empire in India its historians transformed the name into Imaos and Emodus. Alexander Cunningham, 1854, was the first explorer to define Himālaya for the purposes of modern geography. His definition was that the Great Himālaya formed the natural boundary between India and Tibet.

As geographical knowledge progresses it may become necessary to modify or extend an original definition. The two names Himālaya and Tibet represent contiguous mountainous regions, which merge into one another, and it has not been possible to define the boundary line between them with absolute precision.

In his book on Tibet, Sir Thomas Holdich, following Sir Richard Strachey (1880) wrote, "Modern geography restricts the Himālaya to that portion of the "mountainous region between India and Tibet which is enclosed between the "arms of the Indus and Brahmaputra." This definition served its purpose for many years, but in 1913 Morshead discovered the peak of Gyala Peri (23,460 feet) situated on the Great Himālayan alignment outside and beyond the bend of the Brahmaputra, and this discovery obliges us to accept a modification in detail though not in principle of the Strachey-Holdich definition.

In 1904 the surveys of Ryder and Wood in Southern Tibet showed that the whole Tsangpo Valley belonged geographically to Tibet, and in 1908 Sven Hedin confirmed this view; so that the Himālayan-Tibet boundary has now to be retired southwards from the actual line of the Tsangpo river to the small Ladākh range which forms the Nepāl-Tibet watershed. In western Tibet it is not possible to assume the Ladākh range as the geographical boundary, because the Indus is flowing southward of the range. The actual valley of the Indus along its southern bank clearly belongs to geographical Tibet, whilst the highest Himālayan slopes clearly belong to the Himālaya range. The only modification here in the Strachey-Holdich definition that seems in 1931 to be desirable is to place the Himālayan-Tibet boundary upon the Zāskār range, which runs between the Indus river and the Himālayan crest-line and is parallel to both.

THE HIGH PEAKS OF ASIA.

The Great Himālaya range exceeding 1,500 miles in length has had to be subdivided for purposes of geography into different sections, and these sections have been named from the countries with which they are associated, in accordance with the geographical precedents of the Alps and Andes. The sectional names are Punjab Himālaya, Kumaun Himālaya, Nepāl Himālaya and Assam Himālaya. These names have been founded upon custom and tradition: they were chosen in 1907 by Sir Henry Hayden and myself in consultation with political and scientific authorities. They have met with general acceptance, and we recommend their continuance. The name Punjab Himālaya had long been recognised in the Punjab Hill States, and it is a bond of union between mountains and plains: the Punjab Himālaya feed all the Punjab rivers from the Sutlej to the Indus, and these same rivers have brought prosperity to the province. The name Sikkim-Himālaya is not a suitable name for one of the main geographical divisions of the Himālaya. Sikkim owes its importance to Kānchenjunga and Darjeeling: the presence of a single mountain, even Kānchenjunga, is not a sufficient reason for a separate classification, and it is more correct scientifically to regard Kānchenjunga as the eastern peak of the Dhaulāgiri-Mount Everest section (see Part I, Charts I to V,) than to classify it as a solitary and independent mountain. The area of Sikkim is small and its population is made up of Tibetans, Lepchas and Nepālese. The name Sikkim is Lepcha. (See Part I, Chapter 3).

NAMES OF HIMĀLAYAN PEAKS.

Nanda Devi and Trisūl.

Nanda Devi (Goddess Nanda) and Trisūl (trident) are ancient Sanskrit names that are attached to Himālayan peaks in Kumaun and Garhwāl. Trisūl has been so named from its irregular summit, and is supposed to resemble a trident, which is regarded by the Hindus as symbolical of the divine triad. The snow-peak of Nanda Devi is an object of veneration to the villagers in the hot plains of Bijnor. At times the wind blows the snow from the peak like smoke, and the people of the plains will say, "The Goddess Nanda is lighting "her kitchen fire." (*Imperial Gazetteer*). Professor F. W. Thomas writes: "It is possible that the mountain of Kumaun was originally known to the Hin-"dus as Nanda, because a mountain of that name is attributed by them in "their cosmography to the Krauncha continent, which probably represents Ku-"maun."

Badrīnāth (Lord of Badri), Kedārnāth (Lord of Kedār = Siva), Gosainthān (Place of a Saint), and Gauri Sankar (The Goddess and her Consort) are ancient Sanskrit names which have been transferred from shrines and attached to neighbouring peaks; the latter thus serve as beacons to the pilgrims who are climbing to the shrines. The name Badrīnāth is mentioned in the Rāmāyana.

Jaonli (Sanskrit) is a peak near the shrine of Gangotri; the snow peak of Bandarpūnch acts as a beacon to pilgrims visiting the shrine of Jumnotri.

SRIKĀNTA.

Srikānta is the name of a Himālayan peak standing near the source of the Bhāgīrathi branch of the Ganges. It is a well-known mountain and has been an object of admiration to residents of Mussoorie for generations. There has been a general idea that the name Srikānta must have originated from the Hindustāni word Kānta, which has been supposed to be descriptive of the "sharp point" of this peak. Professor F. W. Thomas, C.I.E., writes, "Srikanta is a designation of Siva, 'glorious throat,' referring doubtless to "his blue neck, which gives him also the name Nilakantha. The word "Sri-Kanta, 'beloved by Sri, (Laksmi)' or 'lovable through distinction' is a "good Sanskrit form, and is actually used as a designation of Vishnu."

MAKĀLU.

The name Makālu is a corruption of the name Kamālu. General Bruce was the first to point out that this name Makālu, the origin of which had been frequently discussed for eighty years, was derived from Kamālung, the name of a local river (*Twenty Years in the Himālaya, 1910*). An officer who was recruiting Gurkhas subsequently confirmed General Bruce. The name Makālu has now an historic place in geography and cannot be changed. Its corruption was involuntary and was due to the surveyors' honest effort to represent the Tibeto-Nepālese pronunciation. The two last letters of the word Kamālung were almost silent in pronunciation, there was no emphasis on the first syllable, and the force of the middle syllable led to the inversion Makālu. General Bruce learnt the name Kamālung from Tibetans. In 1867 Colonel Montgomerie was given the name Sihsur for the peak by Indians resident in Nepāl.

NANGA PARBAT.

Nanga Parbat; Sanskrit name, Nagna Parvata, naked hill; or Ananga Parbata, hill of Karna. Nanga Parbat is the Kashmīri name; the regional name is Diamar or Daryāmur or Diamarai (Bruce), and this regional name is applied to the mountain locally. The mountain as seen from India is known by its Kashmīri name. The name Nanga Parbat though of Sanskrit origin is not a name of great antiquity like Badrināth or Kedārnāth; it was probably given to the mountain by Kashmīri pandits in comparatively recent times.

TAKHT-I-SULAIMĀN.

The Persian name Takht-i-Sulaimān, the throne of Solomon, is attached to a conspicuous rocky hill near the Jhelum in Kashmīr, and also to a mountain (height 11,300 feet) situated beyond the Indus, west of the Punjab. The name probably originated during the Mughal empire, and this probability gives to it a certain historic interest, because the Mughal emperors did not give names to the mountains of India.

The Hindu temple situated on the Takht-i-Sulaimān in Kashmīr is very much older than the name Takht-i-Sulaimān itself, and the Hindu name of the hill is Gopadri. The Emperor Akbar built a fort upon the Hari Parbat ridge near the Takht, and he probably introduced the name Takht-i-Sulaimān into Kashmīr. The Amīr Tīmūr, one of the "conquerors of the world," was an ancestor of Akbar, and the early Mughal Emperors must have often visited Tīmūr's tomb at Samarkand. In Lamb's History of Tīmūr we read (*Tamerlane*, p. 97). "The Amīr Tīmūr was always glad to see the snow peak, the Majesty "of Solomon, gleaming through the mists that rose from the Amu river." The traditions of Tīmūr were venerated by the Mughals, and when Akbar saw the hill in Kashmīr enveloped by the mists from the Jhelum, he would have recalled Tīmūr's palace on the Amu Darya.

The name Takht-i-Sulaimān is also attached now to the peak that stands to the west of the Punjab; this name is however not in use among the local Pathān tribes who inhabit the Zhob, Wazīri and Baluchi hills; they call the mountain Kaisargarh. The people of the Punjab plains who see "the snow "peak gleaming through the mists" that rise from the Indus know the mountain as the Takht-i-Sulaimān.

MOUNTAIN NAMES IN SOUTHERN TIBET.
Kailās.

The mountain Kailās is famous in Sanskrit literature as the Paradise of Siva. The name Kailās is so old that it is futile now to seek for its origin or derivation. Professor F. W. Thomas writes, "In Sanskrit we do not profess "to know the etymology of Kailāsa, which is found in the Mahābhārata." Sven Hedin has said (*Trans-Himalaya, II*) that Kailās is "incomparably the "most famous mountain in the world: Mount Everest and Mont Blanc cannot "vie with it."

The actual circuit round the holy mountain is about twenty-five miles and occupies three days. Old men and women, Buddhists as well as Hindus make the pilgrimage. ("*Western Tibet and the British Borderland*," by C. A. Sherring, *1906*).

The first Europeans to visit Kailās were William Moorcroft and Hyder Hearsey in 1812. They entered Tibet by the Niti pass, called by Moorcroft the Niti Ghāt.

In 1731 D'Anville published his map of Tibet and showed Kailās upon it under the Tibetan name of Kentaisse. This was probably a corruption of Kang-tise. In 1828 Klaproth in his map of Tibet used the name Gang-dis-ri, which may have been a corruption of Gang-tise-ri. In the Tibetan dictionary of Sarat Chandra Das the mountain is called Tise.

In 1904 Ryder gave the Tibetan name as Kang-rim-poche.

In "Southern Tibet," Vol. III, Sven Hedin wrote that the Tibetan Lāmas who now live at Kailās "do not know the name Kentaisse: they call the moun-"tain Kang-rim-poche." This name Kang-rim-poche is also given by Sir Charles Bell, and is now accepted as the Tibetan name.

Gurla Mandhāta.

In 1853 Henry Strachey showed this mountain under the name of Gurla. Richard Strachey gave the name as Gurla (Mandhāta). It is now known as Gurla Mandhāta, and in 1904 Ryder found its Tibetan name to be Memo-nam-nyim-ri.

Gurla Mandhāta is a Sanskrit name and Professor Thomas has given the following etymology:—Gurla is a corruption of Guru Deva, and Mandhāta is the legendary Indian monarch Māndhāta who is famous among both Indians and Tibetans.

Gurla Mandhāta is a sacred mountain of the Hindus and stands twenty miles north of the shrine of Khojarnāth. Although it is the highest peak standing north of the Himālayas in Tibet it does not appear to be regarded by the Tibetans as one of their important mountains.

An interesting description of Gurla Mandhāta and of its surroundings and approaches is given by Mr. C. A. Sherring, I.C.S. and Dr. Longstaff in the former's book on "Western Tibet and the British Borderland."

Riwo Phargyul.

This mountain is of exceptional geographical interest; it is standing in close proximity to the deep gorge which the river Sutlej has cut through the Zāskār range, and by means of which this river escapes from the Tibetan highland.

Riwo Phargyul is not one of the sacred Buddhist mountains, but its name is well-known to the Tibetans. It was introduced into modern geography in 1821 by the explorer Alexander Gerard, who called it, not incorrectly, Mt. Purgeool. In 1863 its position and height were determined by the Survey of India, who discovered it to be a double peak and who gave to it the name of Leo Porgial. Colonel Morshead pointed out in 1920 that the more correct name is Riwo Phargyul, and this latter form has been accepted in this book. Riwo is merely one of the Tibetan forms of Ri, mountain, and Phargyul is another variant of Gerard's Purgeool and the Survey's Porgial. Very little was known of the Tibetan language in 1863, when the Survey made their maps of this part of Tibet. Leo may appear in writing to be very different from Riwo, but the Tibetan pronunciation vacillates between the two versions. Tibetan names appearing upon maps are frequently not in accord with local pronunciations or with the forms given by modern travellers. But it is inadvisable to assume that the original field surveyor must have been wrong. Different Tibetans pronounce names differently among themselves and at different times, and even the Tibetan linguists of to-day write names differently among themselves and at different times. Questions of nomenclature can only be determined by a qualified and pains-taking enquirer, and as such a man requires a knowledge of surveying and also of different dialects and peoples, he has to possess exceptional mental powers. Our surveyors have occasionally been criticised for their spellings of names when the errors attributed to them have been due to changes in methods of transliteration.

Chomo Lhāri (formerly spelt Chumalhari).

This mountain is with the single exception of Kailās the best known of the mountains of Tibet, not only to the Tibetans themselves but to European geographers. Sir Charles Bell has written (*Tibet: Past and Present, p. 14*) "Chomo "Lhāri, the mountain of the goddess, is devoutly worshipped." Mr. Sherring has written (*Western Tibet*) "a pilgrimage to the three holy mountains, Kailās, "Gauri Sankar and Chomo Lhāri confers on the devotee a virtue which cannot be "excelled."

This mountain was shown on the Chinese Lāma's survey of Tibet in 1711 and upon D'Anville's map in 1733. It was shown upon all Klaproth's maps compiled from Chinese sources, 1828 to 1836. (Sven Hedin's *Southern Tibet, Vol. III.*) Klaproth gave its height as 26,000 feet, a value too great by 2,000 feet. The error in the Chinese estimate of height is evidence of the impressive appearance of the peak and of its conspicuous prominence, standing as it does in comparative isolation.

Namcha Barwa.

This high mountain of the Assam Himālaya was not introduced into modern geography until 1912, when it was observed by Captain Morshead from the Mishmi hills and by Captain Oakes and Captain Field from the Abor country. They determined its height as 25,445 feet. Colonel Robertson had intersected the peak with his plane-table some years before from the Mishmi side but had been unable to fix it. In 1913 Morshead discovered the Tibetan name for this peak, Namcha Barwa, and this name he said means "lightning burning in the "sky".

The discovery of its great height came as a surprise to geographers, who had been led to think that no peaks above 20,000 feet could be standing north of Assam. The inability of the Survey to observe this peak in former years was due to the fact that it had been completely hidden by comparatively high outer ranges from the observers in Assam. Survey parties had not then been allowed to penetrate the outer hills, which formed a continuous wall blocking the view from the south. It was only owing to the expeditions into the Abor and Mishmi countries which were sanctioned in 1912 that Namcha Barwa came to be observed from two different directions (see Part II, Assam Himālaya). The discovery of its height by Oakes, Morshead, and Field, all officers of the Royal Engineers and of the Survey of India, is the most important advance in Himālayan geography since 1855, when the height of Nanga Parbat was discovered. Of the three discoverers, Capt. Oakes died of wounds received in action in France in 1916, Capt. Field was killed in action in France in 1916, and Colonel Morshead was shot in Burma in 1931.

The discovery of Namcha Barwa and of its great height has led to the prolongation of the crest-line of the Great Himālayan Range for 300 miles. In 1913, one year after the discovery of Namcha Barwa, Captains Morshead and Bailey discovered the gorge by which the Tsangpo river escapes from Tibet through the Great Himālayan range. This gorge had, of course, been known to resident Tibetans for centuries, but the discovery of its exact position had since 1884 been one of the principal objects of geographical exploration in Asia. It was only in 1884 that Kishen Singh definitely proved that the Tsangpo river flowed into the Brahmaputra and not into the Irrawaddy, but Kishen Singh did not discover the place where the river actually left the plateau.

When the first edition of this book on Himālayan Geography was being written in 1907, neither the peak of Namcha Barwa nor the gorge of the Tsangpo had been discovered. The following extract from the first edition is introduced here to illustrate the views that were held in 1907 :—The Sutlej in issuing from Tibet pierces the border range of mountains within 4½ miles of Leo Pargial, the highest peak of its region ; the Indus when turning the great Himālayan range passes within 14 miles of Nanga Parbat, the highest point of the Punjab Himālaya ; the Hunza river cuts through the Kailās range within 9 miles of Rakaposhi, the supreme point of the range. It will form an interesting problem for investigation whether the Brahmaputra of Tibet has cut its passage across the Assam Himālaya near a point of maximum elevation.

It will be seen that in 1907 the existence of a high peak near the gorge of the Tsangpo was considered probable. The fact that such a peak has now been discovered standing near the gorge tends to confirm the view that the peak and the gorge were closely related in their origin. See the first edition of this book, 1907, part III, pages 159 and 186.

The mountain Namcha Barwa may have been known to the Lāma surveyors of 1711 ; a temple named Tchamca is shown in the position of Namcha Barwa inside the bend of the Tsangpo in D'Anville's map. D'Anville's drawing shows, however, that the lāmas had no idea that Namcha Barwa was an important mountain. They do not even draw it as a mountain, and they may have learnt of the temple Tchamca from hearsay.

MOUNTAIN NAMES IN BALTISTĀN.

Many of the names in the Karakorum, such as Gasherbrum and Baltoro and Rimo, have given rise to discussions for years: the more they are examined and analysed, the more certain do we become that all these names are Tibetan. This conviction is becoming so obvious that our successors will probably wonder why there should have been any discussion at all. The people who live in the valleys of the Balti-Karakorum are Tibetans speaking a Tibetan dialect (Balti). But there are Turki-speaking races on the north, Kashmīris on the south, Dardic races on the west: the peak of Nanga Parbat was given its name by people living at a distance from it who were regardless of its local name, and it has been felt that the name Gasherbrum may have originated from a distance too. The ethnography and languages of Western Tibet have not hitherto been clearly understood: the facts that the Baltis are Muhammadans and do not conform to the Buddhist fashions in dress and hair have led to the mistaken belief that they are not Tibetans. The conclusion that is being forced upon us is that all the Karakorum names Gasherbrum, Masherbrum, Baltoro, Biafo, Hispar, Siachen, Rimo, and others are Tibetan (Balti dialect).

Fifty years ago the belief was held that the nomenclature of Northern and Central Tibet was Turki. (See Language Map, Tibet, 1880, prepared for the House of Commons: the Turki language is shown extending across Tibet from the Kunlun almost to Kailās and Mānasarowar). Sven Hedin's maps show Tibetan names. This misconception arose because explorers had recruited the head-men of their parties from Turkistān and had relied on them for geographical names. Colonel Montgomerie, when he made his surveys of Western Tibet, was alive to the danger in obtaining Balti and Hunza and Ladākhi names from Kashmīri surveyors. Our experience of his maps has shown that he was eminently successful in his endeavours to derive all geographical names from the local villagers.

The names Gasherbrum and Masherbrum were introduced into geography by Montgomerie in Baltistān. Neither Moorcroft, nor Henry Strachey nor Cunningham showed these names in their maps of Ladākh.

As our understanding increases, we find internal proofs that the Karakorum names are Tibetan: the glacier name Ri-mo is pure Tibetan. In the glacier name Chogo Lungma, the word Lungma is pure Tibetan. The Tibetan name Chomo Lungma has been proposed for Mount Everest. Lungma is entered over fifty times in each of Montgomerie's maps of Western Tibet (Atlas quarter sheets 45 N. W. and 45 N. E.).

Outside Tibet we do not meet with twin names like Gasherbrum and Masherbrum, differing from one another in their initial letters only. In South India we have Bangalore and Mangalore, but these cities are separated by a great distance, and have no connection with one another. Gasherbrum and Masherbrum are companion peaks: the Baltoro and Saltoro glaciers are both in the Balti-Karakorum. Montgomerie referred also to the Nobundi and Sobundi glaciers. In the Punjab Himālaya we have the Tibetan names for two close companion peaks, Ser and Mer, called also Nun and Kun.

Bishop Peter of the Moravian Mission in Western Tibet has written: "Gasherbrum and Masherbrum have always interested me for their strange "names. One man from Baltistān gave it as his opinion that brum meant "something like the first morning light on a mountain, and the first two syllables "seemed to denote to his mind something like lucky or pleasing. But ety-"mology without a very full knowledge of more than the language is extremely "misleading sometimes. And names of mountains are not at all part of every-"body's knowledge amongst mountain people. They do not come into the "small talk of the villages."

In 1907 Dr. Longstaff gave the name Teram Kangri to a new peak he had discovered in the Karakorum at a place known as Teram. Dr. Longstaff completed the mountain's name by affixing the Tibetan word for snow mountain, namely Kangri.

The Peak K^2.

The highest peak of the Karakorum, named by Colonel Montgomerie K^2 and still known as K^2 had been given no name by the Balti Tibetans. There is nothing surprising in this omission. To them it is merely one of the many points of an immense snowy range, and the fact that it was higher than the other points was unknown to them. The fact moreover that this point was higher than the others would probably not have been of any great interest to them, probably of no more interest than it would be to forest-people to know the highest tree of their forest.

The great altitude of peak K^2 was not discovered till 1856-1858. Colonel Montgomerie first observed the peak from the Kashmir mountain of Haramukh in 1856. His theodolite tent was at a height of 16,000 feet; as a rule an observer cannot tell at the time of his observations which particular peak is higher than the others, as their relative distances are unknown to him. But the Survey tradition has been that when Montgomerie first intersected K^2 from the summit of Haramukh, he turned to his Indian recorder, who was with him, and said, "Babu, we have shot the giant."

Many names have been proposed for this peak K^2;—Mount Waugh and Mount Albert were considered in 1860; Mount Montgomerie and Mount Godwin Austen were suggested about 1886; Mount Akbar and Mount Bābar were names considered in 1905-06. But none of these names met with general approval in India. So the peak of K^2 has continued to be known as K^2 for 70 years. The unforeseen has now happened.

Since 1860 surveyors and sportsmen have been telling their followers that the high peak is named K^2, and from the followers the name has been filtering through to the inhabitants. During the last decade explorers have been finding that the Tibetans of Baltistān are turning the symbol K^2 into a geographical name Kaytoo or Kaychoo. The sound of K^2 in English speech may have reminded them of some word or name in their own language. Dr. Francke, the Moravian missionary, has been the leading authority on the Balti dialect of the Tibetan language, and he was a geographical enthusiast (1900-1910). He never mentioned the possible development of such a name as Kaytoo, but he was one of those who used to explain to the people that the Survey called their peak K^2. The name Kaytoo is a product of local evolution, and it possesses originality, a quality that was lacking in the personal names proposed by geographers.

The following extract is from a letter written in 1931 by the Tibetan scholar Dr. Ribbach, who lived for many years as a Moravian missionary in Western Tibet :—

I have to confess my ignorance in the case of Masherbrum and Gasherbrum.

Biafo may be the Balti form of bya-po, the Tibetan for cock.

Rimo is a Tibetan word and means "picture" (also streaks, which may be suggestive of the crevices).

Baltoro may be derived from dpal-gtor-po, the spreader of abundance, which would be suggestive of the glacier, the giver of fertility.

Saltoro would be "gsal-gtor-po," the giver of light, descriptive of the glacier glittering in the sun.

No doubt these names have in the course of time altered in form and sound so much that it is difficult, even impossible, to trace their origin. But often educated natives (in Tibet at least) know the original form and use it in writing. A few examples :—

Leh, the capital of Ladākh, is "slel" in writing.

Shay, a village near Leh, is "shel" in writing.

Lama Yuru, a monastery in Ladākh, is "Lama-gyung-drung" in writing.

Spituk, a well-known monastery, is "dpe-tub," and so the educated Tibetan spells these names quite differently from the pronunciation.

MOUNTAIN NAMES IN DARDISTĀN.

Boyo-haghurdonas (Boiohaghūrduānasir).

Boyo-haghurdonas is a mountain name that was evolved from the Burushaski language. Colonel Lorimer sees in it three Burushaski words:

Boyo = a divine animal.
Haghur = horse.
Donas = one who opens.

The meaning of the united name,—devil—horse—opener,—is not clear.

The Burushaski language has presented an unsolved linguistic and ethnographic problem: it is the only Indian language that has not been placed by Sir George Grierson in one or the other of the linguistic families. Grierson believes that the Burushaski people are a remnant of aborigines, probably Dravidian, who were cut off from the other aboriginal inhabitants of India by the Aryan invasions, and who have found a sheltered home amongst the hills of Hunza for forty or fifty centuries.

HARAMOSH.

The name Haramosh comes from the Shina language, and Colonel D. L. R. Lorimer writes that the second vowel is long and stressed. There is, however, an emphasis on all three syllables. The name has no connection with the Kashmīrī mountain name Haramukh (*Grierson's Kashmiri Dictionary, p. 343*) in which the second vowel is short or lacking (Harmukh). In Kashmīrī, Hara is a name of the God Siva and Haramukh means the face of Siva. Colonel Lorimer writes, "The proposal to call the ridge that carries Rakaposhi the "Haramosh ridge is sound. Haramosh is a well-known name, but Rakaposhi "is not. A traveller can always easily ascertain by enquiry where Haramosh "is."

The name Haramosh has been derived from haram = bad, and from mosh = man; but Lorimer considers this derivation to be a worthless popular etymology. "Haram," he writes, "is Arabic for forbidden: Mosh is the Khowār "word for man, and the Khowār language never extended east of Yasin."

RAKAPOSHI.

Colonel Lorimer writes, "Where this name came from is a mystery. The "Mīr of Hunza used always to twit us, the British, for having invented it. "The correct name of this mountain, as known in Hunza, is Dumani. I "have never been able to imagine that it was a European invention, and I am "quite prepared to believe that it is a genuine native name." The Mīr of Hunza was mistaken in attributing this name to the British. It was introduced into modern geography in 1854 by Henry Strachey, whose geographical names have always been found by subsequent surveyors to be correct. The explorer Vigne introduced the name Haramosh in 1835: Henry Strachey in 1854 showed on his map the three names Haramosh, Rakaposhi and Dubanni. In 1860 Colonel Montgomerie of the Survey of India found all three of Strachey's names known to the inhabitants, and in 1884 Colonel Tanner found the name Rakaposhi to be known in Gilgit. Colonel Tanner painted the picture of this mountain that was published as the frontispiece to Black's History of the Indian Surveys, 1891, and he introduced the idea that Rakaposhi meant Devil's Tail. The tradition grew in the Survey of India that Rakaposhi was a Sanskrit name,

But there was no foundation for this view; Sir George Grierson has written, "Raka may be a corruption of Rakhas, a devil; but if Rakaposhi means devil's "tail, it must only be corrupt Hindustāni, as poshi must be the Hindustāni "pūnch. In Dardistān posh means covering or dress. It looks as if the "meaning Devil's Tail had been invented by a Kashmīri surveyor or clerk."

The following extract is from a letter written in 1930 by Lieutenant G. C. Clark, R. E.:—" Rakaposhi is called Dumani by the people of Hunza and "Nagir, and this means a Necklace of Clouds. Rakaposhi is a name more "used by the people of Gilgit, and is said to be derived from Raka the name of a "lad and from Poshi, a Shina word. The tale goes that Raka was a Gilgiti "from the Bagrot nullah, who was in league with the fairies. Every now and "then he went off with some of them to some distant spot. One day he dis-"appeared and did not return for some time. When he did get back, he told "the villagers in reply to their questions that he had been taken up to the top "of the hill and from there had seen most of the world. Hence the name, which "means in the Shina language Raka's View Point."

There is a general consensus of opinion amongst surveyors and linguists that the name Rakaposhi is a valuable geographical name, and that it must certainly be retained; the tradition of its Sanskrit origin and of its supposed meaning "Devil's Tail" must however be abandoned. The name Rakaposhi is undoubtedly Shina. Colonel Lorimer criticises Lieutenant Clark's etymology on the grounds that Raka is not a Shina name and is not given to lads in Gilgit.

Dubanni.

The third name of the Hunza triplet is Dubanni or Dubunni. There has been a suspicion that this name might have been a corruption of the Shina name Dumani, but investigations have shown that this is not the case. Henry Strachey has been proved right in his adoption of Dubanni. The name Dubanni is quite well-known to the local inhabitants and has been heard in use in the Haramosh district by many surveyors and travellers. It is said to mean a "blanket of clouds," the first syllable "du" being traced to the Shina word "dum" meaning "smoke". But this popular etymology is said by Colonel Lorimer to be mere conjecture.

Kunjut and Hunza-Kunji.

In Tables IV, V and VI of Chapter I three peaks will be found named Kunjut and three named Hunza-Kunji. These six peaks were observed from long distances many years ago. The northern border of Hunza was not then so well-known as it is now; the original observers probably thought that all these peaks were standing upon the Hunza border; we now know that whilst some are situated actually on the border, a few stand inside it, as the Hunza river has cut back through the Karakorum range and forced the Hunza watershed to retire behind the crest-line of peaks. The name Kunjut (modern spelling Kanjut) is the Central Asian or Turcoman name for Hunza: Colonel Lorimer writes that the name Kanjut is used for Hunza by the Chinese officials. Dr. Neve mentions in his book "Thirty years in Kashmir," 1913, that the village head-men in Hunza told him that the Muztāgh Pass was formerly used by Kanjuti raiders and had to be closed for that reason.

The 3 peaks now named Kunjut do actually stand upon the Hunza border Montgomerie had in the first instance called them "Trans-Indus," a name suggestive of distance and uncertainty. When it was discovered that they were standing in the Kanjut region, they were re-named Kunjut.

For the other three peaks the name Hunza-Kanjuti would probably have been more correct than Hunza-Kunji; until surveyors have learnt the dialects spoken by a population of mixed races, they are apt to miss syllables cut short in speech, and mispronunciations lead to misspellings. The name Hunza-Kunji denotes the Hunza-Kanjut border, just as in Europe we speak of the Franco-German border.

The peak names Kunjut and Hunza-Kunji have thus been evolved from the intercourse of Indian and Kashmīri surveyors with Dard and Kunjuti residents, there is nothing artificial about these names, and they are distinctive and descriptive. They have been found most useful for many years. The practice of grouping a small number of peaks under one name has been found to be successful in such cases as Gasherbrum and Tirich Mīr.

The Name Hindu Rāj.

In the wild Trans-Indus country south of Dardistān there is a mountain range named Hindu Rāj.

General Bruce has questioned the suitability of this name. General Bruce knows the Himālaya from Sikkim to Dardistān and in his book, "Twenty years in the Himālaya," he has often been helpful in his references to nomenclature and maps. When therefore on a rare occasion he does give way to an outburst of criticism, his words carry weight. General Bruce says that the name Hindu Rāj is hopeless, and he asks, why Hindu? why Rāj? These questions cannot be answered. But their author, under the influence of the mysticism which pervades the mountains, goes on to say that the Hindu Rāj range itself would be annoyed, if it only realised the unsuitability of its name. If however we could consult the range, I feel that it might possibly say to us, "My name Hindu Rāj is a relic of former greatness. Don't deprive me of it. "I once belonged to an ancient kingdom." (Possibly Gandhāra, of Vedic times.) (The Hindu Rāj range is described in Chapter 25.)

NOJLI TOWER
A STATION OF THE GREAT TRIGONOMETRICAL SURVEY BUILT IN THE PLAINS OF UTTAR INDIA NEAR ROORKEE
AND FROM WHICH THE HIMALAYAN PEAKS OF BADRINATH, KEDARNATH, JAONLI AND BANDARPUNCH HAVE BEEN OBSERVED

CHAPTER 5.

ON THE ERRORS OF THE ADOPTED VALUES OF HEIGHT.

(i) THE PROBLEM AS VIEWED IN 1907.

The values of height given in Tables I to VII of this paper must be accepted with caution; some are more reliable than others, but none are correct to a foot, and many investigations will have to be completed before altitudes can be determined with a greater degree of accuracy than at present.

Errors of observation.—All observations are liable to error; no telescope is perfect, no level is entirely trustworthy, no instrumental graduations are exact, and no observer is infallible.

In ordinary triangulation the objects to be observed are sharp and specially erected signals, but for the observations of a high peak, the summit, however ill-defined, cannot be furnished with a suitable mark.

If a flat-topped peak be observed from a near station, the surveyor runs the risk of mistaking some lower point for the summit, the latter being obscured from his view by an intervening shoulder.

Errors of measurement however can be greatly reduced and rendered practically negligible, if a peak be observed with a good theodolite on *several* occasions and from *different* stations; observations of Mount Everest, of K^2, of Kānchenjunga, and of others have been repeated so often and from so many different places that the local angles of elevation have been probably determined within one or two seconds of the truth, and the errors in the mean values of height *due to faults of observation* are probably less than 10 feet. But in the cases of peaks Nos. 19 and 40 of Table IV, and others, which have been observed from one station only and on but few occasions from that, errors due to faults of observation may attain to 100 feet. A single intersection of a peak from a single station deserves no weight whatever: it may give a result hundreds of feet in error.

The adoption of an erroneous height for the observing station.—Heights in the Himālaya that have been measured from one or two stations only may in places be thrown into error to the extent of 10 or 15 feet by the adoption of erroneous altitudes for the stations of observation.

In the case of the Karakorum and Ladakh ranges the liability to error on this account is larger and is perhaps 30 feet; the peaks of the Hindu Kush have been observed from less known stations than those of the Karakorum and are possibly 70 feet in error in consequence.

The Kāshgar range being still more remote from the triangulation of India, the heights of its peaks are less reliable than those of the Hindu Kush; and the peaks of Kungur and Muztāgh Ata may be in error by 300 feet, or even more, on account of the accumulation of error in the assumed altitudes of the stations from which they have been observed.

Variations of snow.—An element of uncertainty is introduced into heights by the fact that the altitudes of peaks are always varying in nature with the increase and decrease of snow. The discrepancies that obtain between the different determinations of height of the same peak may be partly due to the fact that some observations have been made after the snow has been accumulating, and others after it has been diminished by heat, evaporation, wind, and avalanches. All heights on land have to be measured from the surface of the sea, and as the latter rises and falls with the tides, a mean level of the sea has to be adopted; and so in the case of the great peaks, we shall have eventually to assume the mean level of the snow at their summits as the altitude to be determined.

The deviation of gravity from the normal.—A plumb-line is a string supported at its upper end and stretched by a weight attached to its lower end.* If there were no irregularities of matter near the earth's surface a plumb-line would hang truly normal; but mountains exert a lateral pull, and tend to deflect it towards them. In the same way as plumb-lines are pulled out of the normal, so is the surface of water near mountains pulled out of its spheroidal form. The attraction of the great mass of the Himālaya and Tibet pulls all liquids towards itself, as the moon attracts the ocean, and the surface of water in repose assumes an irregular form at the foot of the Himālaya. If the ocean were to overflow northern India its surface would be deformed by Himālayan attraction. The liquid in levels is similarly affected and theodolites cannot consequently be adjusted; their plates when levelled are still tilted upwards towards the mountains, and angles of elevation as measured are too small by the amount the horizon is inclined to the tangential plane. At Darjeeling the surface of water in repose is inclined about 35″ to this plane, at Kurseong about 51″, at Siliguri about 23″, at Dehra Dūn and Mussoorie about 37″.

No attempt has yet been made to apply corrections to the values of height on account of Himālayan attraction; the determinations of the deflections of the

---

* To render intelligible references to the deviation of gravity it is necessary to define the following words, *vertical, horizontal, normal, level, tangential.* If the earth had been at rest, it would under the influence of gravity have assumed the form of a sphere; its rotation round an axis has converted the sphere into a spheroid flattened at the poles. The present figure of the earth is not a perfect spheroid, however, as the surface is disfigured by mountains and valleys, which are rigid enough to withstand the influences of gravity and rotation. Everywhere in fact on land we meet with slopes and cliffs that are obviously inclined to the general surface of the earth. Water, however, whether it be in a basin, or lake or ocean, conforms closely to the spheroidal surface, and it is more exact to say that the figure of the sea is a spheroid, than that the figure of the earth is one. The surface of the sea, however, though more nearly spheroidal than that of the land, suffers from slight irregularities, and water in repose does not conform exactly to the spheroid. Continents and mountains attract water towards themselves, and their attraction disfigures the surfaces of oceans and ponds and levels. If the earth were a homogeneous and perfect spheroid, the direction of gravity would everywhere be perpendicular to its surface, but the earth is irregular, and gravity does not always coincide with the perpendicular to the general surface. Gravity acts in a direction perpendicular to the surface of water. We have then to consider what we mean by a *vertical* line—whether it is the perpendicular to the earth's mean surface or whether it is the direction of gravity. The word *vertical*, we think, should be employed to describe the direction of gravity; the line perpendicular to the mean surface should be called the *normal*. The actual surface of the sea and of water, however disfigured from a spheroid, is the *level* surface, and the word *level* should only be applied to this actual surface. The following definitions will explain the difference between the *horizontal* and *tangential* planes at any point of the earth's surface: the *horizontal* is the plane that is tangential to the local surface of water, however the latter may be deformed; the *tangential* plane is the plane that is tangential to the mean spheroidal surface.

plumb-line are at present not sufficiently perfect to justify the results being utilised to correct altitudes. (*Philosophical Transactions of the Royal Society of London:* Series A, Volume 205 (1905), pp. 289 to 318.)

We know that all angles of elevation to Himālayan peaks measured from the plains of India and from the outer hills are too small, and consequently all our values of Himālayan heights are too small. Errors of this nature range from 40 to 100 feet.

Of the deflection of gravity from the normal in Tibet or Kāshgar or on the Karakorum or Hindu Kush we know as yet nothing.

If a peak be observed from different directions, the deflection of the plumb-line in the plane of the peak will probably be different at every observing station, and the several values of height may consequently appear discordant. Such discordances, however, are unavoidable; their presence implies that the direction of gravity has been varying, and it leads us to hope that the errors due to deflections of the plumb-line are tending to cancel in the mean.

Atmospheric Refraction.—The most serious source of uncertainty affecting values of heights is the refraction of the atmosphere. A ray of light from a peak to an observer's eye does not travel along a straight line, but assumes a curved path concave to the earth. The ray enters the observer's eye in a direction tangential to the curve at that point, and this is the direction in which the observer sees the peak. It makes the peak appear too high. Refraction is greatest in the morning and evening and least in the middle of the day; it is different in summer from what it is in winter. If we observe Dhaulāgiri from the plains of Gorakhpur, it appears to fall 500 feet between sunrise and the afternoon, and to rise again 300 feet before sunset. Even in the afternoon, when it appears lowest, it will still be too high by perhaps 700 feet.

In 1853 Sir Andrew Waugh determined the curvature of the path of a ray of light between the outer Himālaya and the low plains of Bengal, by means of simultaneous observations taken from both ends of the ray. He then assumed that the path of a ray to a snow peak would be similarly curved, and he reduced the apparent heights of the peaks accordingly. But we believe now that he reduced the heights by too much: his determination of a ray's curvature in the outer Himālaya was correct, but this curvature, we think, is not maintained at higher altitudes. As the rarefaction of the atmosphere increases, the ray assumes a less curved path, and Sir Andrew Waugh's method attributed to refraction a greater effect than it really has. To the Karakorum heights Colonel Montgomerie employed smaller corrections for refraction than Waugh used for the Himālaya.

Summary of errors.—If we bring together in the following table the different errors to which carefully determined heights of peaks are liable it will help to focus our ideas:—

TABLE VIII.—Magnitudes of possible errors.

Source of error.	Great Himálaya range.	Karakoram range.	Káshgar range.
Variations of snow-level from the mean	Unknown	Unknown	Unknown.
Errors of observation	10 feet	20 feet	100 feet.
Adoption of erroneous height for observing station	10 feet	30 feet	300 feet.
Deviation of gravity	60 feet, too small	Unknown	Unknown.
Atmospheric refraction	150 feet, too small	10 to 30 feet	50 feet.

Deduction of the height of Mount Everest.—The following table shows how the different values of the height of Mount Everest have been deduced:—

TABLE IX.—Height of Mount Everest.

Station of observation.	Year of observation.	Height of station of observation.	Distance from Mount Everest.	Values of height, if no correction for refraction be applied.	Resulting height as determined by Waugh with co-efficients of refraction varying from 0·07 to 0·08 from stations in the plains.	Resulting height from computations in 1905 with coefficient of refraction 0·05 from stations in the hills.	Resulting height with assumed coefficient of refraction 0·0645 from stations in the plains.
		Feet.	Miles.	Feet.	Feet.	Feet.	Feet.
Jaroi	1849	220	118·661	30366	28991·6	..	29141
Mirzapur	1849	245	108·876	30165	29005·3	..	29135
Janipati	1849	255	108·362	30141	29001·8	..	29117
Ladnia	1849	235	108·861	30171	28998·6	..	29144
Harpur	1849	219	111·523	30221	29026·1	..	29140
Minai	1850	228	113·761	30282	28990·4	..	29160
Suberkum	1881	11641	87·636	29576	..	29141	..
Do.	1883	11641	87·636	29572	..	29137	..
Tiger Hill	1880	8507	107·952	29860	..	29140	..
Sandakphu	1883	11929	80·666	29620	..	29142	..
Phallut	1902	11816	85·553	29589	..	29151	..
Senchal	1902	8599	108·703	29941	..	29134	..
Mean	..	..	..	..	29002	29141	29141
Range of variation in values*	..	..	..	794	Misleading.†	17	43

The 5th column gives the values of height obtained from observation, if no correction for refraction be applied. It will be noticed that all the values of height in this column derived from observations taken at low-lying stations exceed 30,000 feet, whereas those derived from observations taken at high altitudes are less than 30,000 feet.

The reason of this difference is that refraction tends to elevate a peak to a greater extent when the observation is made through the thick atmosphere of the

---

* The range of variation is the difference between the largest and smallest values of height in the column above; it is the maximum discordance obtained, and as such it furnishes evidence as to the correctness of the refraction coefficient adopted.

† The extent of the range of variation affords no useful information unless the same value for refraction has been employed throughout. By using selected values of refraction we can make all values of height identical and have no range of variation at all.

plains than when the line of sight passes only through the rarefied air of hill stations. It will be noticed that when no correction for refraction is applied, the largest of the values in the 5th column differs from the smallest by 794 feet, but that the application of corrections reduces the discrepancies materially.

The height 29,141 is still probably too small, as it has yet to be corrected for the effects of deviations of gravity. Though it is a more reliable result than 29,002, the latter value is still to be retained in maps and publications of the Survey. We cannot claim to have solved the problems of refraction, nor to have eliminated all uncertainties: our knowledge of the deflections of gravity is still but superficial, and although we may endeavour continually to improve our heights, it would be a mistaken policy to introduce new values at every step of the investigation. Values of heights, as has been explained in a previous section, furnish means of identification and are not to be altered frequently or without good reason. We have discussed the height of Mount Everest to show the degree of uncertainty attaching to it, but we do not propose to substitute 29,141 for the long adopted and well-known value 29,002. (*Survey of India, Professional Paper No. 9, 1905*).

Deduction of the height of Kānchenjunga.—It is probable that the accepted height of Kānchenjunga is, like that of Mount Everest, too small: the following table shows how the height has been deduced:—

TABLE X.—Height of Kānchenjunga.

Station of observation.	Year of observation.	Height of station of observation.	Distance from Kānchenjunga.	Values of height, if no correction for refraction be applied.	Resulting height as determined by Waugh with co-efficients of refraction varying from 0·07 to 0·09 from stations in the plains.	Resulting height from computations in 1905 with coefficient of refraction 0·05 from stations in the hills.	Resulting height with assumed coefficient of refraction 0·0645 from stations in the plains.
		Feet.	Miles.	Feet.	Feet.	Feet.	Feet.
Daundāngi	1847	307	84·951	28856	28137·8	..	28224
Thakurganj	1847	264	88·491	28948	28138·3	..	28266
Bandarjūla	1847	238	92·560	29060	28128·6	..	28312
Minai	1850	228	115·174	29494	28162·5	..	28346
Baisi	1850	234	115·631	29483	28152·1	..	28322
Harpur	1849	219	124·694	29651	28133·7	..	28297
Sonebai	1847	8599	50·158	28401	28138·8	28231	..
Birch Hill	1847	6874	44·907	28379	28152·3	28239	..
Tonglu	1847	10073	46·369	28370	28169·6	28220	..
Observatory Hill	1884	7162	45·720	28353	..	28212	..
Mean	..	..	..	..	28146	28226	28295
Range of variation in values*	..	..	..	1298	Misleading.†	14	122

* The range of variation is the difference between the largest and smallest values of height in the column above; it is the maximum discordance obtained and as such it furnishes evidence as to the correctness of the refraction coefficient adopted.

† The extent of the range of variation affords no useful information unless the same value for refraction has been employed throughout. By using selected values of refraction we can make all values of height identical and have no range of variation at all.

If we examine the results of the 5th column, which have not been corrected for refraction, we find that all the heights derived from observations at low-lying stations exceed 28,800 feet, and all those derived from observations made at high altitudes are below 28,410. The heavy atmosphere of the plains had greater refracting effects than the rarefied air of the hills and raised the peak to a greater extent.

If no correction for refraction be applied, the values of height vary from 28,353 to 29,651, a discrepancy of 1298 feet: the 7th and 8th columns show how this discrepancy can be reduced by corrections for refraction.

Deduction of the height of Dhaulāgiri.—The following table shows how the height of Dhaulāgiri was obtained: no observations have been taken to it from stations in the hills:—

TABLE XI.—Height of Dhaulāgiri.

Station of observation.	Year of observation.	Height of station of observation.	Distance from Dhaulāgiri.	Values of height, if no correction for refraction be applied.	Resulting height as determined by Waugh with co-efficients of refraction varying from 0·07 to 0·09.	Resulting height with assumed coefficient of refraction 0·0645.
		Feet.	Miles.	Feet.	Feet.	Feet.
Morairi	1848	334	105·975	27974	26791·0	27002
Banarsia	1849	329	95·625	27928	26773·8	27128
Saunbarsa	1849	315	104·943	28093	26830·8	27151
Purena	1849	299	105·800	28011	26813·1	27044
Ghaus	1849	327	95·812	27852	26775·5	27052
Tulsipur	1848	376	104·461	27930	26824·8	26988
Anârkali	1848	434	137·340	28640	26756·6	27002
Mean	..	..	..	..	26795	27052
Range of variation in values *	..	..	..	788	Misleading.†	163

The height 26,795 is too low: the reductions made on account of refraction were too great.

The observations in the North-west Himālaya of the great peaks of K^2, Nanga Parbat, etc., were taken not from low dusty hazy plains as those of the Nepālese peaks were, but from high stations, and the rays passed through a rarefied atmosphere.

---

* The range of variation is the difference between the largest and smallest values of height in the column above; it is the maximum discordance obtained and as such it furnishes evidence as to the correctness of the refraction coefficient adopted.

† The extent of the range of variation affords no useful information unless the same value for refraction has been employed throughout. By using selected values of refraction we can make all values of height identical and have no range of variation at all.

THE HIGH PEAKS OF ASIA.

Deduction of the height of K^2.—The height of K^2 was deduced by Colonel Montgomerie as follows :—

Table XII.—Height of K^2.

Station of observation.	Year of observation.	Height of station of observation.	Distance from K^2.	Values of height, if no correction for refraction be applied.	Resulting height as determined by Montgomerie with co-efficients of refraction varying from 0·04 to 0·05.
		Feet.	Miles.	Feet.	Feet.
Shangruti	1859	17531	78·9	28640	28246·6
Biāchūthūsa	1859	16746	99·0	28846	28218·7
Marshāla	1858	16906	58·6	28472	28240·0
Kāstor	1858	15983	66·0	28560	28261·4
Thurigo	1858	17246	61·8	28515	28254·1
Harāmukh	1856	16001	136·5	29300	28293·9
Kanāri-Nār	1857	15437	114·3	28920	28218·4
Bārwāi	1857	16304	88·0	28666	28258·5
Thalanka	1857	16830	74·7	28613	28322·7
Mean	..	..	..	..	28253
Range of variation in values *	..	..	..	828	104

Deduction of the height of Nanga Parbat.—The following table shows the height of Nanga Parbat as deduced from the observations using different refraction coefficients :—

Table XIII.—Height of Nanga Parbat.

Station of observation.	Year of observation.	Height of station of observation.	Distance from Nanga Parbat.	Height with refraction coefficients of										
				0·00	0·01	0·02	0·03	0·04	0·05	0·06	0·07	0·08	0·09	0·10
		Feet.	Miles.	Feet.	Feet.	Feet.	Feet.	Feet.	Feet.	Feet.	Feet.	Feet.	Feet.	Feet.
Ahartātopa	1855	13029	133·744	27885	27646	27407	27168	26929	26689	26449	26210	25970	25734	25494
Pahārgarh	1855	11356	118·751	27680	27492	27304	27116	26923	26739	26551	26362	26174	25988	25800
Gogipatri	1855	7752	95·055	27332	27211	27090	26969	26848	26726	26604	26485	26363	26243	26124
Har. mukh	1856	16001	59·275	26882	26835	26788	26741	26694	26647	26599	26552	26505	26460	26413
Kāzi Nāg	1856	12111	73·559	27028	26956	26884	26812	26740	26669	26595	26524	26452	26380	26307
Poshkar	1856	8323	83·491	27219	27125	27031	26937	26843	26749	26654	26562	26468	26376	26282
Ismāīl-di-dori	1856	12630	65·805	26947	26892	26837	26782	26727	26671	26617	26563	26508	26454	26400
Safāpur	1856	10296	66·339	26917	26858	26799	26740	26681	26624	26564	26506	26447	26387	26329
Hānt	1856	13479	43·167	26771	26746	26721	26696	26671	26646	26621	26596	26572	26546	26522
Menganwār	1856	8715	50·510	26854	26811	26768	26725	26682	26638	26596	26553	26510	26467	26425
Mārināg	1856	11814	46·342	26780	26751	26722	26693	26664	26636	26606	26579	26549	26520	26492
Mean	..	..	..	27118	27029	26941	26853	26764	26676	26587	26499	26411	26323	26235
Range of variation in values.*	..	..	..	1114	900	686	475	265	125	265	386	602	812	1023

* The range of variation is the difference between the largest and smallest values of height in the column above; it is the maximum discordance obtained and as such it furnishes evidence as to the correctness of the refraction coefficient adopted.

It will be noticed that when a coefficient of 0·10 is used, the height of Nanga Parbat as determined from different places varies between 25,494 and 26,522, a range of 1,028 feet.

This great variation shows that the coefficient of 0·10 is inapplicable: with a coefficient of 0·09 the height varies from 25,734 to 26,546, a range of 812 feet. The range of variation decreases, until with a coefficient of 0·05 all the values of height fall between 26,624 and 26,749, a range of 125 feet. If we decrease the coefficient still further to 0·04, the variations again begin to increase, and the range extends to 265 feet, from 26,664 to 26,929 : if the coefficient be decreased to 0·00 the range of variation becomes 1,114 feet.

The actual height adopted by Montgomerie for Nanga Parbat was 26,620, and we are unable to improve upon his value : it is produced if a general coefficient of 0·057 be accepted for refraction.

The rise of the Himālaya.—Is the great Himālaya range still rising ? This is a question often asked but which no one has been able to answer. The observations of peaks made between 1850 and 1860 were not sufficiently prolonged at any one station to enable us to rely with certainty on the values of height then obtained. When the absolute height of a peak is being measured, stations of observation have to be multiplied in order to cancel the effects of refraction and gravity, but when a slow variation in height is being determined, it is better to carry out long series of observations from one station only. In the latter case differences are being sought, not absolute heights, and all that is necessary is to repeat observations from the same station, on the same days of the year, and under the same conditions. In 1905 a series of observations was commenced from the trigonometrical station of Nojli, and it is proposed to observe the heights of several peaks for some years and at different seasons in each year. If a reliable series of results be once obtained, a similar set of observations can be repeated at a subsequent date and any actual change of height that has occurred in the interim may be discovered.

The Siwālik range was elevated at a more recent date than the Himālaya, and is the most likely of all the ranges to be rising still : a bench-mark has been placed on the crest-line south of Dehra Dūn, and its height has been determined by spirit-levelling : if the bench-mark is preserved, future changes in altitude should be discoverable.

Slow changes in the level of land, unaccompanied by sudden movements, have been observed to occur along many coasts. At great distances from the sea such changes would take place without being noticed : without the aid of the sea as a datum we do not observe slow gradual movements, and a continuous rise of a foot a year might go on for centuries without attracting the attention of man. If an earthquake occurs and a tract of land suddenly subsides along a line of fracture in the crust, the result is apparent and measurable, but if the elevation of a large area takes place in all directions gradually and without fracture of the crust or any marked upheaval it may be considerable and yet escape observation. In the Dharmsāla earthquake of 1905 an immense region may have been elevated or depressed through many feet, but if the change were nowhere sudden we should not without refined trigonometrical observations become aware of its occurrence.

(ii) The Problem as viewed in 1931.

(a) Atmospheric Refraction.

Since 1907 a great advance has occurred in our knowledge of atmospheric refraction, which has been due to the investigations of Dr. de Graaff Hunter (*Professional Paper No. 14*). Hunter has shown that the refraction of a ray depends upon the heights above sea-level of the two stations at the ends of the ray, and upon the temperature and pressure at the station of observation. Instead, therefore, of assuming (as we formerly did) a somewhat arbitrary coefficient of 0·05 at hill-stations and of 0·0645 in the plains, the Survey of India now employs a value which is definitely dependent upon height, temperature and pressure.

The value is obtained from a table and its use results in a considerable increase of accuracy,* provided we always observe as heretofore at the time of minimum refraction. The atmospheric pressure and the temperature lapse rate (or rate of change of temperature with height) are the factors which principally affect the coefficient of refraction. The former can be measured, or estimated with very fair accuracy, whereas the lapse rate cannot, and the latter is the principal source of uncertainty. The table has been calculated on the assumption that the lapse rate is 3°F. per 1000 feet, a value which observation has shown to be fairly typical except in close proximity to the ground.

During the last century many observers, including Sir Andrew Waugh, and many computers, including Radhānāth Sikhdār, devoted their time and thought to the study of refraction. They were well aware of its wild behaviour, of its changeableness, its inconstancy, its distortions and its multiplication of images, but they could find no method underlying its caprices. To all who have been interested in the scientific history of the Survey and who have been aware of the difficulties which it has encountered in obtaining corrections for refraction, it will be a source of satisfaction to feel that the solution of the problem should have at last been discovered, not by investigators in Europe or America, but by researches at Dehra Dūn.

Some knowledge has also been obtained by Hunter's investigations of the variation of the refraction between morning, afternoon and evening. Our knowledge of this variation is not sufficient to justify the deliberate taking of observations in the morning or late evening, but it enables us to utilise old observations which have been made at these hours.

---

* Auxiliary Tables, 5th Edition, Part III, Table 5 Sur.

By making use of this increased knowledge of refraction, and by applying corrections for the deflections of the plumb-line, Dr. de Graaff Hunter has obtained values of 29,149, 28,287, and 27,016 for the heights of Mount Everest, Kānchenjunga, and Dhaulāgiri respectively.

(b) *The Replacement of the Spheroid by the Geoid.*

The following extract is from a paper by Dr. Hunter, dated 1931 :—

The most difficult question of all still remains to be considered. Above what datum are these heights measured ? Are they measured above Everest's spheroid, to the geometrical surface of which all Indian latitudes and longitudes are referred, or are they measured above the geoid, the slightly irregular surface which would be assumed by the surface of the sea, if the sea could be extended into the middle of the continents by small frictionless canals ? The answer to this question is that as they stand the figures refer to neither of these surfaces. The heights given in Tables IX, X, and XI are with reference to various spheroidal surfaces, each with curvature equal to that of Everest's spheroid, but placed so as to be tangent to the geoid at each station of observation. Strictly speaking the result given in each line of these tables is referred to a different datum.

Two datum surfaces have been mentioned above, the geoid and the spheroid. Which of these ought logically to be used ? The answer is that either may be used, provided it is used consistently, with a slight preference for geoidal heights since they are the measure of the amount of effort required to reach the top of a hill, and of the fall available for power or irrigation. In practice the most accurate way of measuring heights, so far as instrumental errors are concerned, is spirit-levelling, and when possible all triangulated heights are adjusted to spirit-levelled heights. Now spirit-levelled heights are geoidal heights, for the bubble in the level is affected by the same influences as the sea-level in the hypothetical canals by which the geoid is defined. We are then forced to the conclusion that the geoid must be accepted as the datum of height.

The heights obtained by ordinary triangulation, with fairly short rays, used without correction for deflection of the plumb-line, are also a fairly close approximation to geoidal heights. But when peaks are fixed by rays 100 miles long, passing over mountainous country in which great deflections occur, the height obtained without correcting for deflection is by no means an accurate geoidal height. Under these circumstances it becomes necessary to obtain a spheroidal height by correction for the deflection, and then to try to estimate the separation between geoid and spheroid under the peak.

The following are probably correct geoidal heights within 50 feet.

Mount Everest	29,050
Kānchenjunga	28,200
Dhaulāgiri	26,925

We can summarise the height of these three mountains as follows :—

	Above an Everest spheroid which coincides with the geoid south of Nepāl.	Above the geoid.
Everest	29149 ± 5	29050 ± 15
Kānchenjunga	28287 ± 2	28200 ± 15
Dhaulāgiri	27016 ± 5	26925 ± 15

CHAPTER 6.

THE GEOLOGY OF THE GREAT PEAKS.

In dealing with the great peaks the geologist is at no small disadvantage as compared with the surveyor, whose instruments enable him to work from a distance and to fix with accuracy the position and height of the object of his observation. The geologist, on the other hand, must toil arduously up the mountain sides, examining at close quarters such outcrops of rocks as he can find clear of snow, and, where further progress is barred, must depend for his information on fallen fragments, splintered from the cliffs above and brought down by avalanches and glaciers to form moraines and talus heaps. Thus the composition of the highest peaks is rarely known in any detail, but the general character of the rocks can be ascertained, with a fair approximation to certainty, from observation of the material on their flanks, and from a distant view of the weathering characters and apparent structure of the peaks themselves: it has thus been found that almost all those of 25,000 feet or more in height are composed of granite, gneiss, and associated crystalline rocks.

Of the granite there are at least two varieties, a foliated rock composed essentially of quartz, felspar, and biotite (black mica), and a younger non-foliated form containing, in addition to quartz and felspar, white mica (muscovite), black tourmaline, beryl, and various accessory minerals. The former variety was long regarded as a sedimentary rock which had been converted by heat and pressure into gneiss, but its truly intrusive nature was recognised by the late Lieutenant-General C. A. McMahon, who proved conclusively that the great central gneissose rock of the Himālaya was in reality a granite crushed and foliated by pressure. [*Records, Geological Survey of India*, Vol. XV (1882), p. 44, Vol. XVI (1883), p. 129, and *Geological Magazine*, Dec. III, Volume 4 (1887), p. 215]. This rock is frequently pierced by veins of the second or non-foliated variety, and where these run parallel to the foliation planes, they lend to the series a deceptive appearance of bedding and cause it, when seen from a distance, to be mistaken for a mass of stratified deposits. This is a common characteristic of the higher peaks and may be noticed in many of the granitic masses of the great Himālayan range.

Although our experience leads us to assume that all the highest peaks are composed largely of granite, many more observations must be made before this can be positively asserted to be the case.

Thus Chomo Lhāri (23,997 feet) is composed of foliated (gneissose) granite penetrated by veins of the non-foliated variety, and flanked by the altered representatives of slates and limestones metamorphosed by the granite which has been forced up through them from below. Further to the west, the Kānchenjunga group is largely formed of gneissic granite, flanked by metamorphic rocks certainly in part derived from pre-existing sediments, but recrystallised by heat and pressure. The double peaks of the Jonsong La, for instance, are part of an inverted outlier of Mesozoic limestones, and the long range further north is composed of the same limestones, uninverted, but overthrust upon granite. [G. O. Dyhrenfurth, "Himalaya," Berlin (1931)].

The Everest group is a pile of altered sedimentary rocks, originally shales and limestones, converted into banded hornfels, finely foliated calc-schists and crystalline limestones, traversed by veins of white muscovite-tourmaline granite. [A. M. Heron, *Records, Geological Survey of India*, Vol. LIV, pt. 2, pp. 233-234, 1922]. These metamorphic rocks dip northward and are believed to pass into, or beneath, the highly folded Jurassic Spiti shales of the Tibetan plateau. Their age may be supposed to be Triassic or Jurassic. Downwards they pass into the banded Himālayan biotite-gneiss, which is intimately penetrated with sills and dykes of the muscovite-tourmaline granite. The gneiss is perhaps intrusive in these metamorphics, but whether it is wholly an igneous rock, or is a composite-gneiss formed by the injection and rolling out of granite veins along the foliation of mica-schists—highly altered, and possibly very ancient, sedimentaries—is as yet uncertain.

The conspicuous broad light brown band of rock, extending along into the base of the final pyramid, from the prominent shoulder, 27,390 feet, north-east of the main peak of Mount Everest, is not however, a sill of granite, as was stated in the account quoted above, but is really calcareous sandstone. [N. E. Odell, *Geographical Journal*, LXVI, pp. 289-315 (1925)]. The final pyramid is composed of dark calc-schist, very compact, dipping northwards at 30°.

Owing to the exclusion of British travellers from Nepāl, we know little or nothing of the geological characters of the peaks in Nepāl.

To the west of Nepāl we are on surer ground, since both Kumaun and Garhwāl have been geologically surveyed. Here again the high peaks, such as Nanda Devi, the Kedārnāth group and Kāmet [C. L. Griesbach, *Memoirs, Geological Survey of India*, Vol. XXIII, (1891), pp. 43, 90, 194], are all composed of granite and gneiss with gneiss and schist on their flanks, while granite is also probably the prevailing rock on Muztāgh Ata and the other high peaks of the Kāshgar range.

Nanga Parbat or Diamir is composed almost entirely of finely schistose, streaky biotite-gneiss with interbedded marbles, graphite-schists, etc., well-stratified, and with a persistent dip to the north-west. These are traversed by thick dolerite sills, now converted into massive amphibolite and hornblende-schist. D. N. Wadia ["Geology of Nanga Parbat, Mount Diamir," *Records, Geological Survey of India*, Vol. LXVI, pt. 2 (1932)] has no doubt that these gneisses are metamorphic products of the pre-Cambrian Salkhala series, which constitutes the surrounding region. Through this para-gneiss complex are intruded sheets and dykes of later gneissic granite and of this the summit of the mountain is largely composed.

Recent work by the Italian and other expeditions in the Karakorum show that sedimentary rocks enter into the architecture of the high peaks of that region to a greater extent than in the cases already cited. The Crystal * and Gasherbrum groups are composed of grey and black limestones with fossils which show them to be Permo-Carboniferous in age [Ardito Desio, *Geographical Journal*, LXXV, No. 5, pp. 402-411, (1930)] while Broad Peak has the same limestones on its eastern side, with, on the north, shales, gneiss, granite and epidiorite with serpentine.

The Golden Throne † region is composed of many-coloured limestones; the peaks of the Skamri range comprise a great sequence of white and grey crystalline limestones, which form the right side of the Drenmang valley and the left side of the Nobundi Sobundi valley.

The north slope of the southern divide of the Baltoro glacier (the Masherbrum-Chogolisa chain) is biotite-gneiss, with dykes of granite, as is the Muztāgh Tower.

The commanding pyramid of K^2 is composed of well-stratified gneiss, with granite dykes cutting through it, with its summit of clear gneiss.

The general sequence in the Karakorum, as described by Ardito Desio, is somewhat similar to that of the Everest region. The basis is light-grey gneiss, occasionally porphyritic, crossed in all directions by great granite dykes; in higher levels the content of biotite increases, giving the gneiss a more pronounced schistosity and a darker colour. Next to these occur very thick shales, passing upwards into limestones interbedded with shales, schists, epidiorites and serpentines. Where metamorphism has been less pronounced, the sedimentaries yield fossils which show them to range in age from the *Fenestella* shales (Middle Carboniferous) to the Trias.

This correspondence between the great elevation and the geological structure of the high peaks appears to be too constant to be attributable to mere coincidence, and we are forced to the conclusion that their exceptional height is due to the presence of granite. This may be explained on two separate grounds, either (*a*) that the superior power of the granite to resist the atmospheric forces tending to their degradation has caused them to stand as isolated masses above surrounding areas of more easily eroded rocks, or (*b*) that they are areas of special elevation.

If now we examine the relationships of the peaks to one another, we find that along certain definite lines the intervening areas are also frequently composed of the same granite as the peaks themselves, and if we follow these definite lines we further find that they constitute the axes of the great mountain ranges. Thus the great peaks lie on more or less continuous and elevated zones composed of granite and crystalline rocks, and since the lower portions of the zones are of the same composition as the peaks themselves, it is difficult to regard the latter merely as relics of a once continuous zone of uniform height, and it seems probable that

---

* Crystal group (19,400 ft.) in the Karakorum lies south-east of K^2 at the junction of the Baltoro and Godwin-Asuten glaciers.

† The Golden Throne (23,600 ft.) is at the head of the Baltoro glacier on its southern divide.

special elevating forces have been at work to raise certain parts of the zone above the general level of the whole; when once such elevation has been brought about, the disparity between the higher peaks and the intervening less elevated areas would undoubtedly be intensified by the destructive forces at work; the mantle of snow and ice, while slowly carrying on its own work of abrasion, will serve as a protection for the peaks against the disintegrating forces of the atmosphere, whilst the lower unprotected areas will be more rapidly eroded.

By the assumption that the higher peaks are due to special elevatory forces, it is not intended to imply that each peak is the result of an independent movement, for it has already been shown in a previous section of this paper that the peaks occur in well-marked clusters, any one of which may cover an area of many hundred square miles: when, therefore, during the development of the Himālaya as a mighty mountain range vast masses of granite welled up from below, forcing their way through and lifting up the pre-existing rocks above, it is probable that owing to dissimilarity of composition and structural weaknesses in certain portions of the earth's crust, movement was more intense at some points than at others, and that the granite was locally raised into more or less dome-like masses standing above the general level of the growing range: these masses were subsequently carved by the process of erosion into clusters of peaks. Whether the elevatory movement is still in progress it is not at present possible to say, but many phenomena observable throughout the Himālaya and Tibet lead us to infer that local elevation has until quite recently been operative, and the numerous earthquakes still occurring with such violence and frequency forcibly remind us that the Himālaya have by no means reached a period of even comparative rest.

APPENDIX 1.

A SYNOPSIS OF THE LINGUISTIC SURVEY OF INDIA.

The volumes of the Linguistic Survey of India by Sir George Grierson were published in 1927, and they are a monument of scientific research. The 723 different languages and dialects of India are divided into three families, the Indo-European, the Mongolian, and the Dravidian. This classification does not agree exactly with that adopted by ethnologists; the latter have classed Europeans and Indians together as Aryans, but in the Linguistic Survey the Indo-European family is divided into two sub-families, the Aryan and the European. The word Aryan has been frequently used in the past as equivalent to Indo-European, and English, Latin and German are sometimes called Aryan languages. Grierson protests against this misuse of the word Aryan, and he only applies it to the eastern branch of the Indo-European family; the English, Latin and German languages are other branches of the same family.

The Aryan sub-family has three divisions, the Iranian, the Indo-Aryan and the Dardic.

Iranian.—The Iranian languages consist of Persian, Pashtu (Afghānistān), Baluchi, and Kurdish, and also of some minor dialects spoken in Chitrāl and the Pāmirs.

Indo-Aryan.—The Indo-Aryan languages include Sanskrit, Panjabi, Sindhi, Marathi, Bengali, Hindi, Gujarāti, Assamese and others. This Sketch of Himālayan Geography and Geology is only concerned with those Indo-Aryan languages which are spoken in the mountainous regions separating India from Tibet, and which are classified by Grierson as the "Pahāri group". Eastern Pahāri is sometimes called Parbatiya, sometimes Gurkhāli, sometimes Khāskhura; it is not spoken outside Nepāl except by soldiers of the Gurkha regiments and the various Gurkha colonies in India. Eastern Pahāri is called Nepāli by Europeans, as though it were the principal language of Nepāl. In Nepāl the principal languages are not Indo-Aryan but Mongolian, the most important being Newāri. Eastern Pahāri is the language of the court in Nepāl, but it has borrowed words from the Tibeto-Burman languages and now presents a mixed character.

Central Pahāri includes the dialects known as Kumauni and Garhwāli; both are written in the Nāgri character.

Western Pahāri is the language spoken in the Himālayas between the Jumna and Kashmīr. It has numerous dialects differing considerably. They are closely related to the languages of Rājputâna and Gujarāt.

Dardic.—The only other Aryan languages in the Himālayas are those known as Dardic. Dardistān is the home of the Dardic languages; it includes Kashmīr, and Gilgit, the Indus and Swāt Kohistāns, Chitrāl and Kāfiristān.

The two principal Dardic languages are the Kashmīri and the Shina, and these are of geographic importance; Shina is the language of Gilgit and of a large area of mountain country between Baltistān and Kashmīr. In former times it extended into Western Tibet, where Francke found traces of it in the place-names, but it has now been superseded there by Tibetan dialects, and old Dard sites on the Indus are now occupied by Tibetans.

Grierson writes that Kashmīri is a mixed form of speech, and that its base is akin to Shina, and that many of its words are of Dardic origin. But Kashmīr has received many immigrants, and for centuries it has been a home of Sanskrit study. The learned Kashmīris themselves regard their language as truly Indian, but Sir George Grierson writes that "no philologist can "have any doubt that Kashmīri has a Dardic basis."

In Hunza-Gilgit there is an aboriginal language, Burushaski, still spoken; it was probably the language of the country 4000 years ago, before the invasion by the Aryan (Dardic) race.

THE MONGOLIAN LANGUAGES.

The Mongolian languages are divided into two sub-families, the Tibetan and the Tibeto-Burman.

The Tibetan languages.—In Tibet itself there are three dialects of Tibetan, namely Central Tibetan, Ladākhī and Baltī. In the Himālayas there are four Himālayan dialects of Tibetan, namely Lhoke (also known as Drukpa) spoken in Bhutān, Da-njong-ka spoken in Sikkim, and Sharpa and Kagate spoken in Nepāl.

The Tibeto-Burman languages.—But there are an older set of Mongolian languages which crossed the Himālayas from the north even before Tibetan was established in Tibet (p. 12). These are the Tibeto-Burman languages; of these there is the Rong language of Sikkim, nicknamed Lepcha by the Nepālese. There are also the Newari, the Murmi, the Sunwar and the Magari dialects of Tibeto-Burman in Nepāl, and 26 other different dialects of Tibeto-Burman also spoken in Nepāl.

In addition to the dialects of Tibeto-Burman spoken in Nepāl, there are five such dialects in Kumaun spoken by races who live between the Pahāri-Indian races and the Tibetans.

There are also some Tibeto-Burman dialects spoken in the hills of Kanaur, of Kulu, of Kangra, of Chamba and of Lāhul.

Assam branch of Tibeto-Burman.—East of Bhutān the hills north of the Brahmaputra, extending beyond the extreme eastern corner of Assam are occupied by five tribes, the Akas, the Daflas, the Miris, the Abors and the Mishmis, each speaking their own dialect of Tibeto-Burman.

THE VOLUMES OF THE LINGUISTIC SURVEY WHICH REFER TO THE HIMĀLAYAS.

The Linguistic Survey of India has been published in 18 volumes, and these deal with the languages which are spoken in all parts of India and Burma. The volumes that deal with the languages of the Himālayas and Tibet are the following:

Indo-Aryan languages.

Vol. I, Part III. Comparative dictionary, Indo-Aryan languages.
Vol. VIII, Part II. Dardic, including Kashmīri.
Vol. IX, Part IV. Pahāri languages.
Vol. X. Iranian family of languages.

Mongolian languages.

Vol. I, Part II. Comparative Vocabulary.
Vol. III, Part I. Tibetan and Tibeto-Burman languages.

CHART I
Peaks of the first magnitude

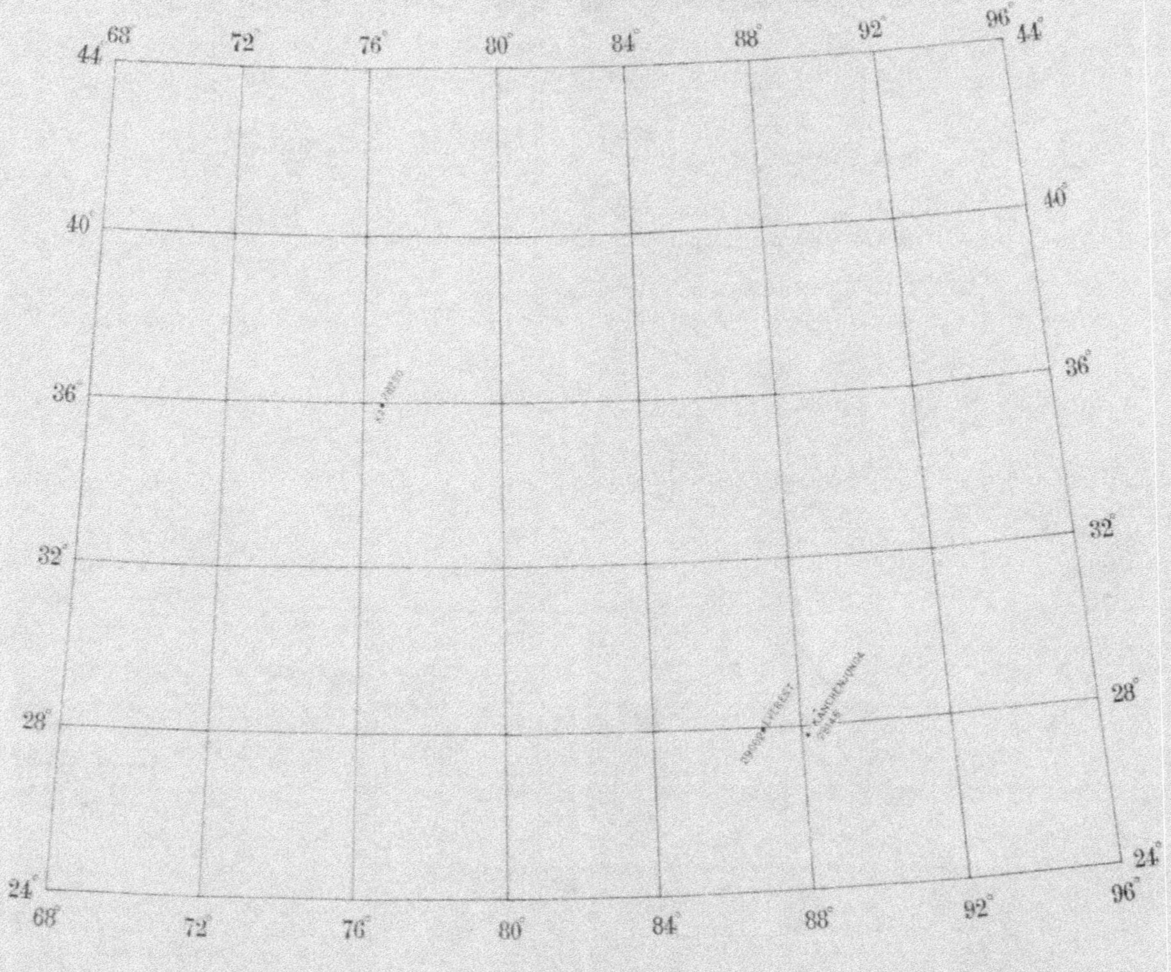

CHART II

Peaks of the second and first magnitude

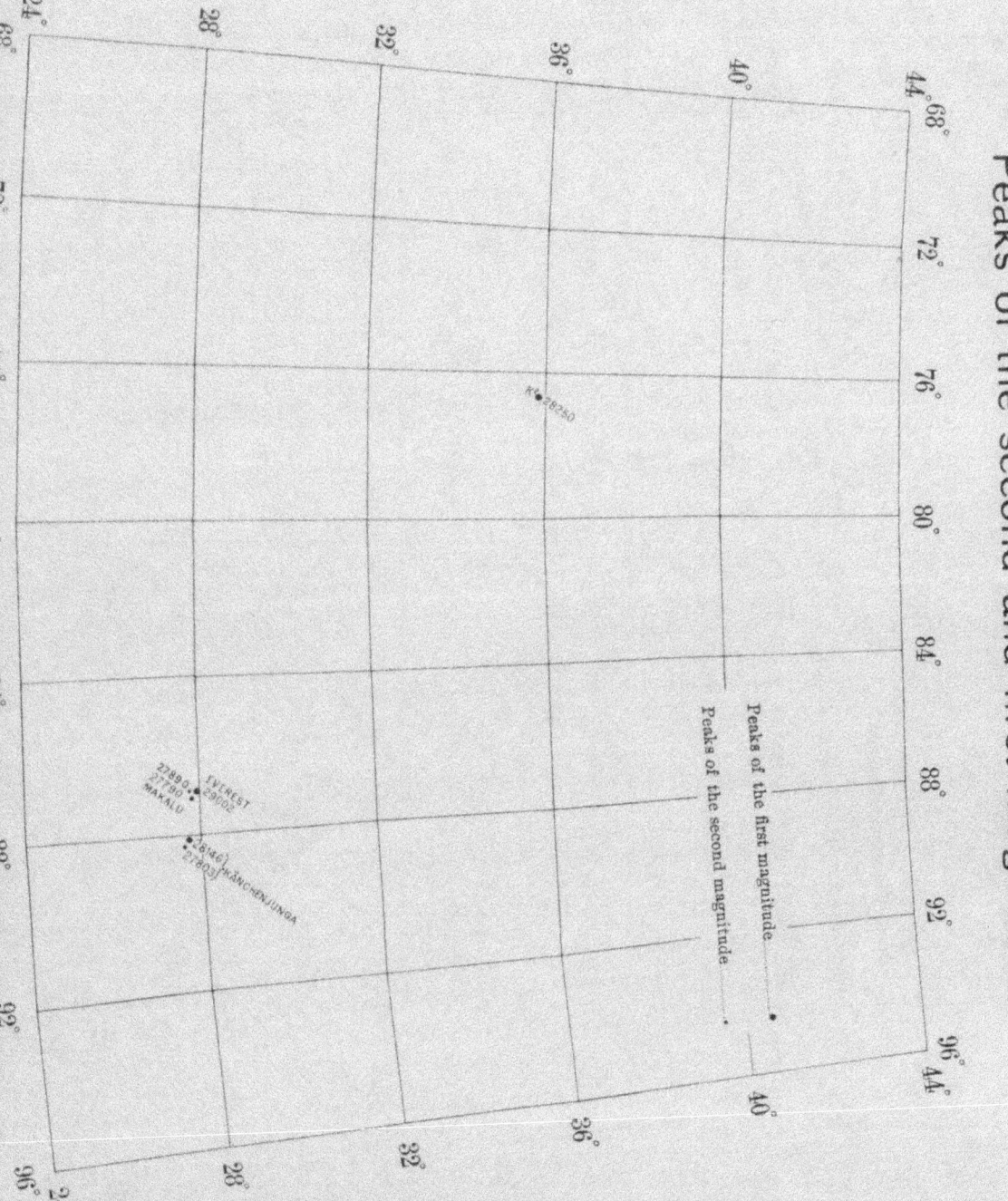

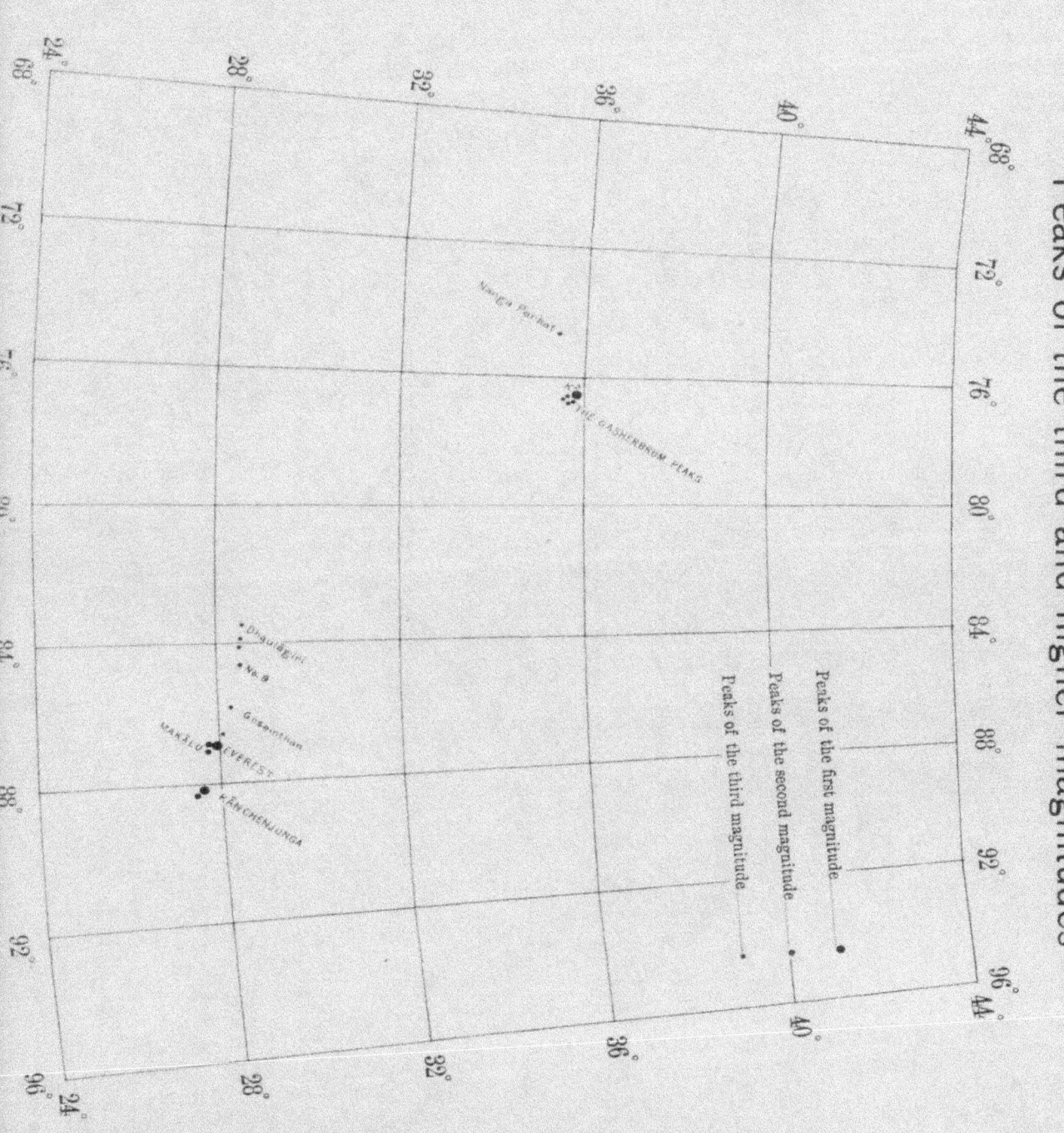

Peaks of the third and higher magnitudes

CHART IV
Peaks of the fourth and higher magnitudes

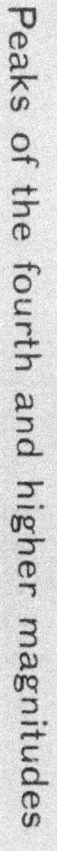

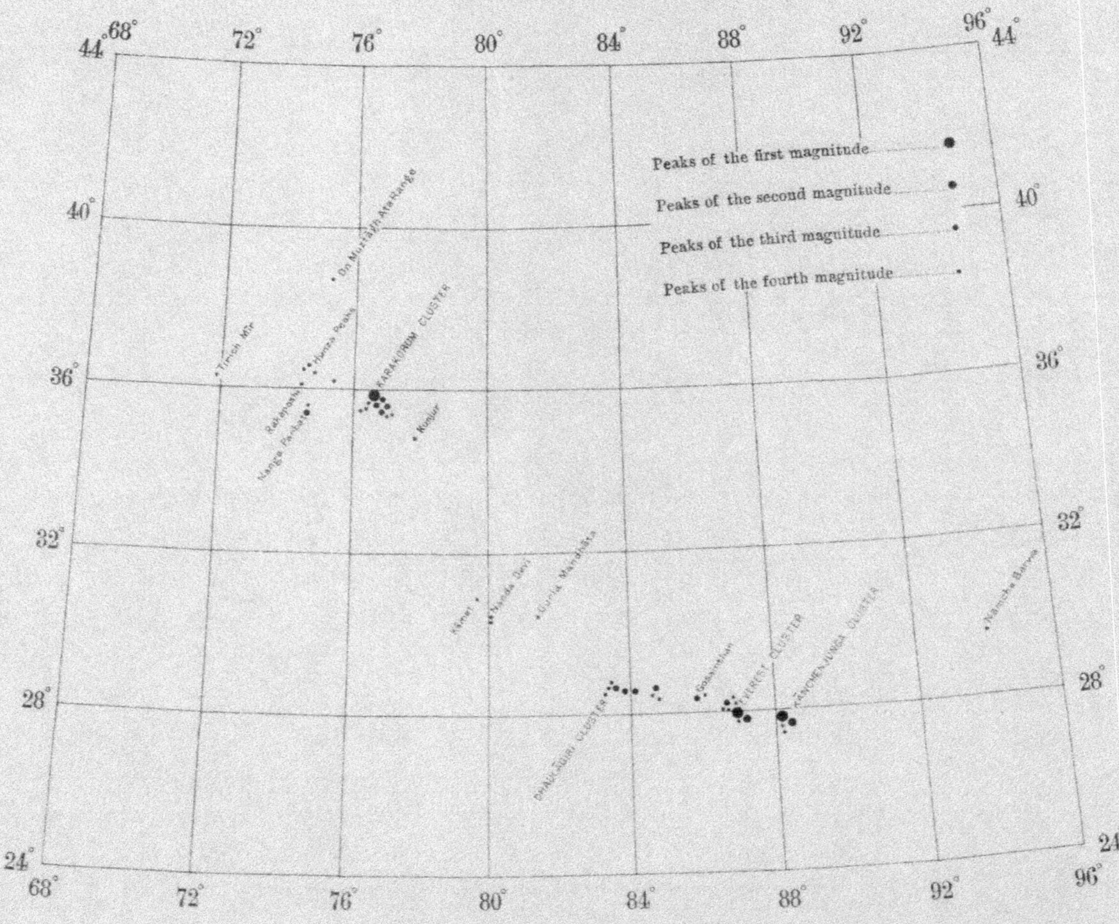

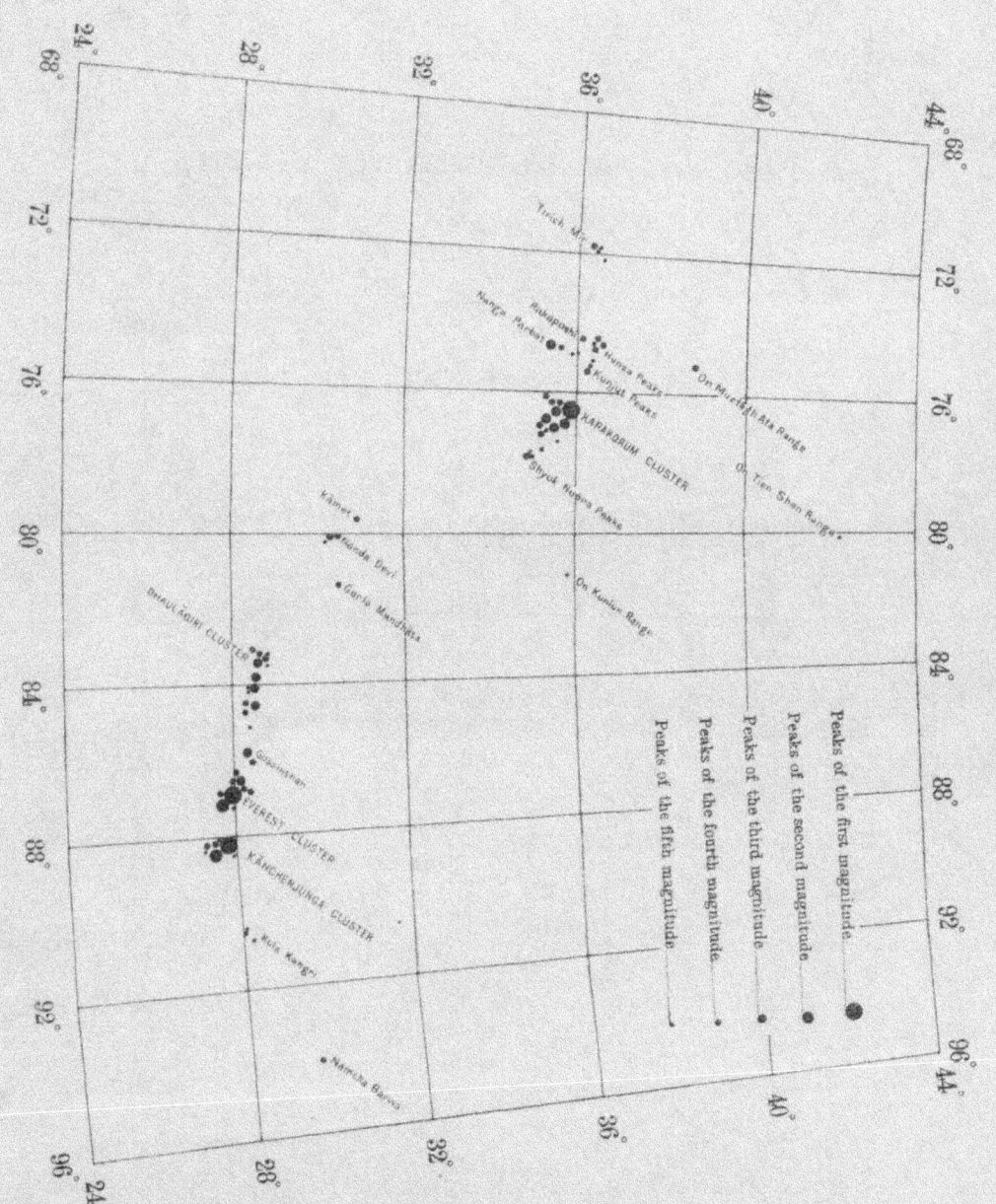

CHART V
PEAKS OF THE FIFTH AND HIGHER MAGNITUDES

Continuation of CHART VI

MAKĀLU and MOUNT EVEREST as seen from Kampa Dzong in Tibet

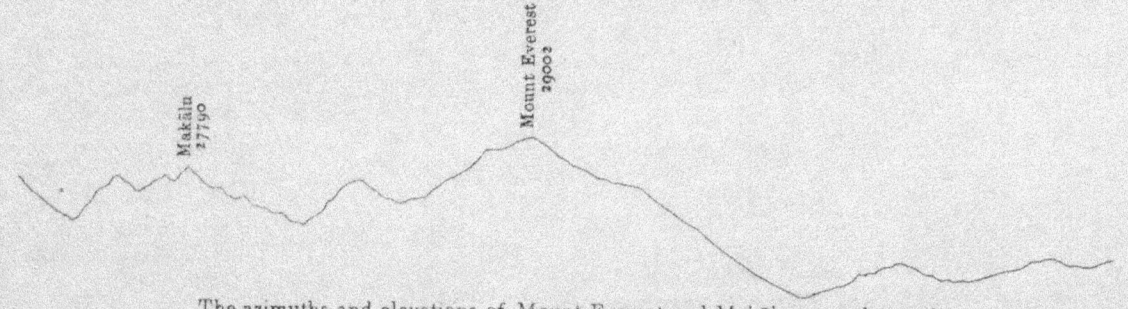

The azimuths and elevations of Mount Everest and Makālu were observed
from Kampa Dzong by Major Ryder in Season 1903-04

MAKĀLU and MOUNT EVEREST
as seen by Captain Wood from Pompa-zu-lung (height 18164 feet) in Tibet

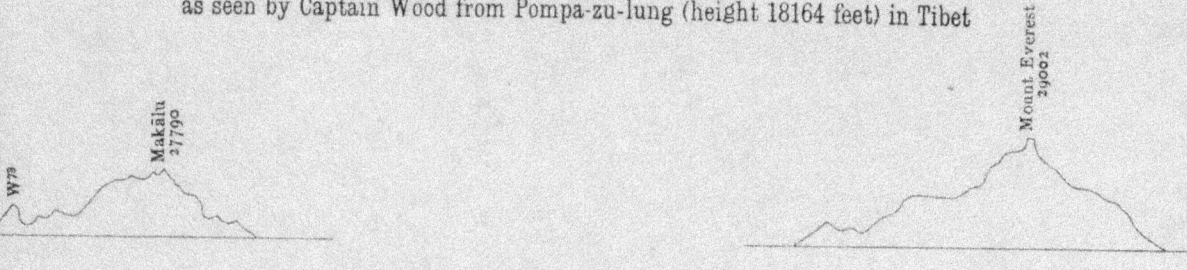

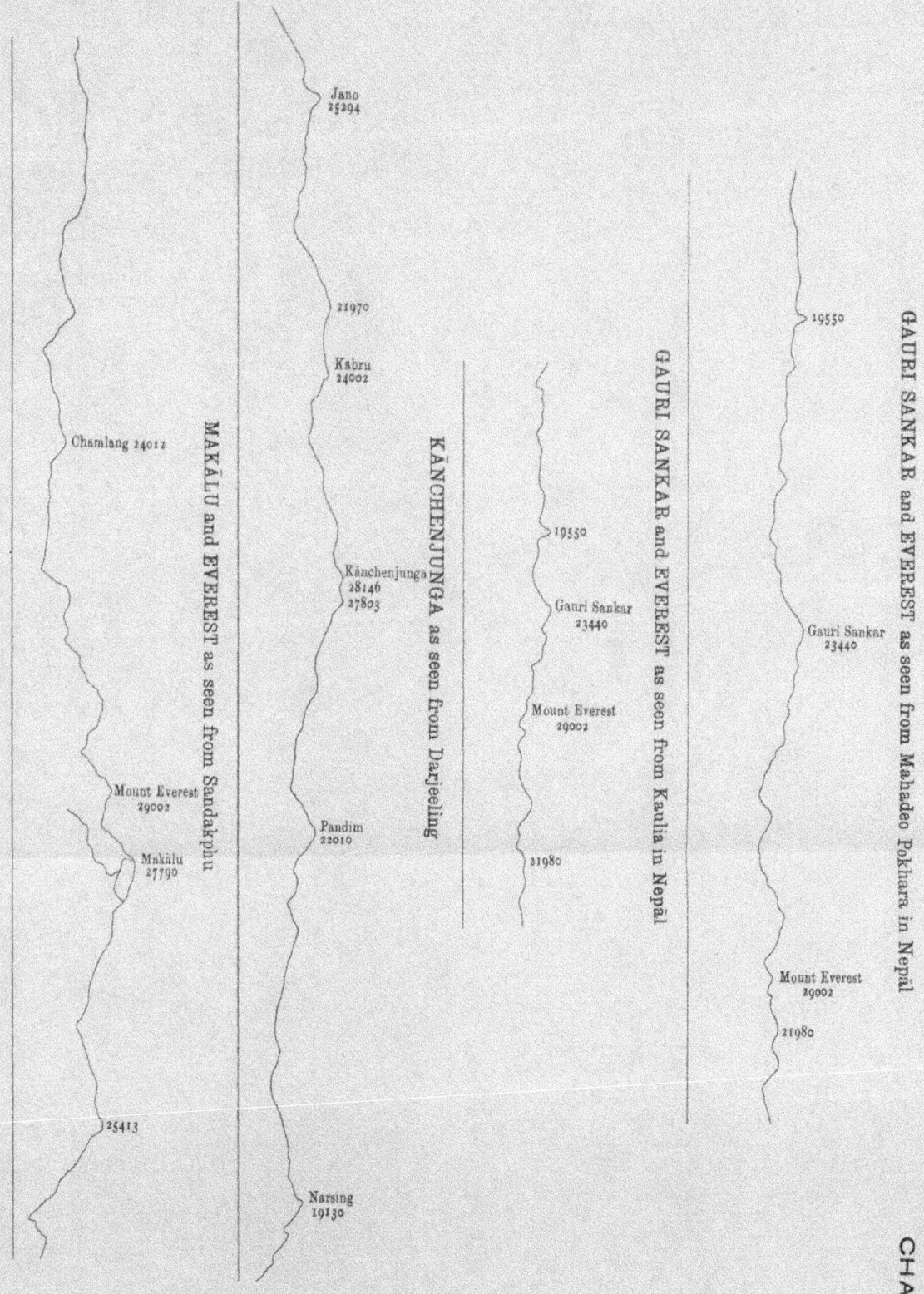

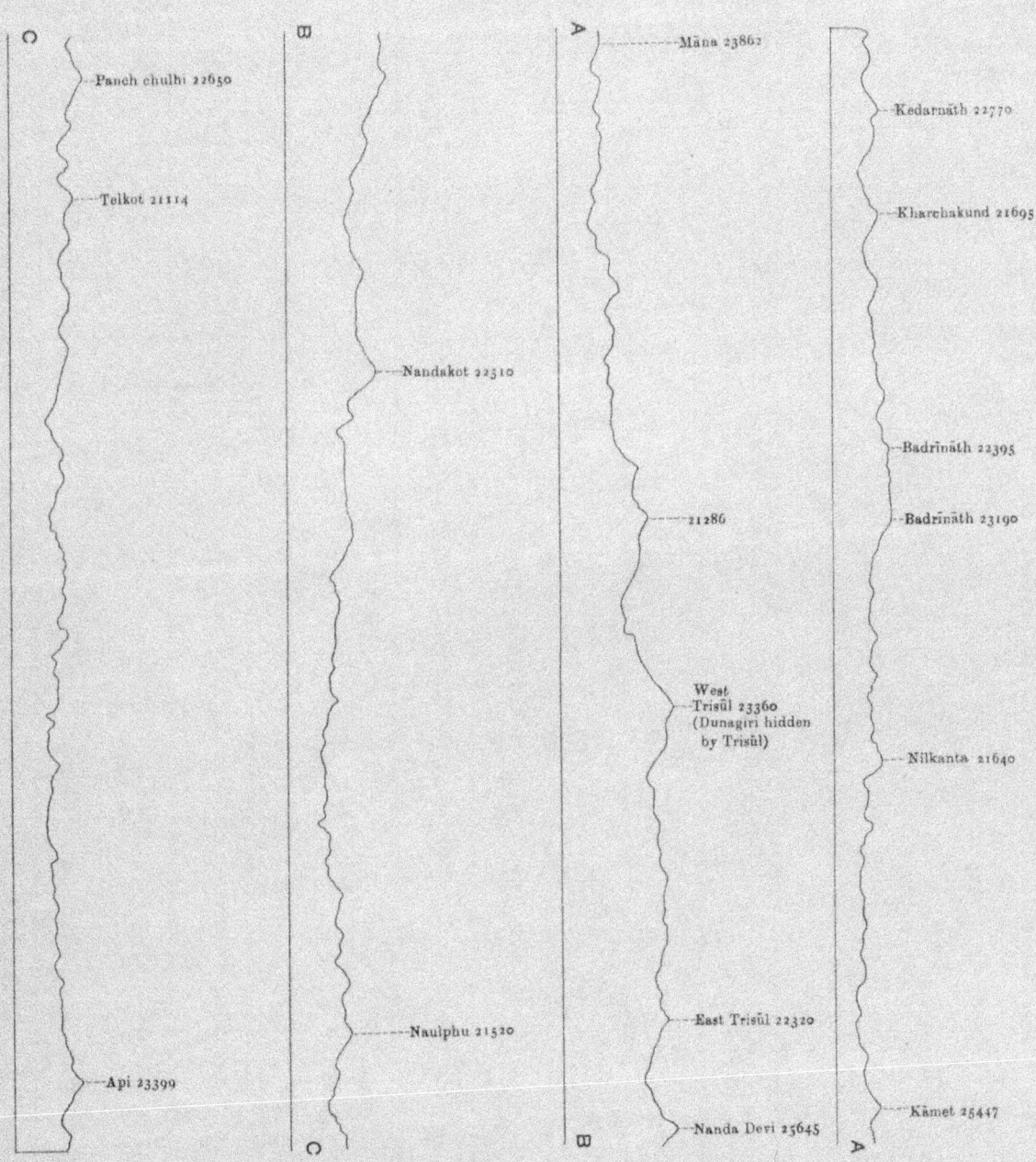

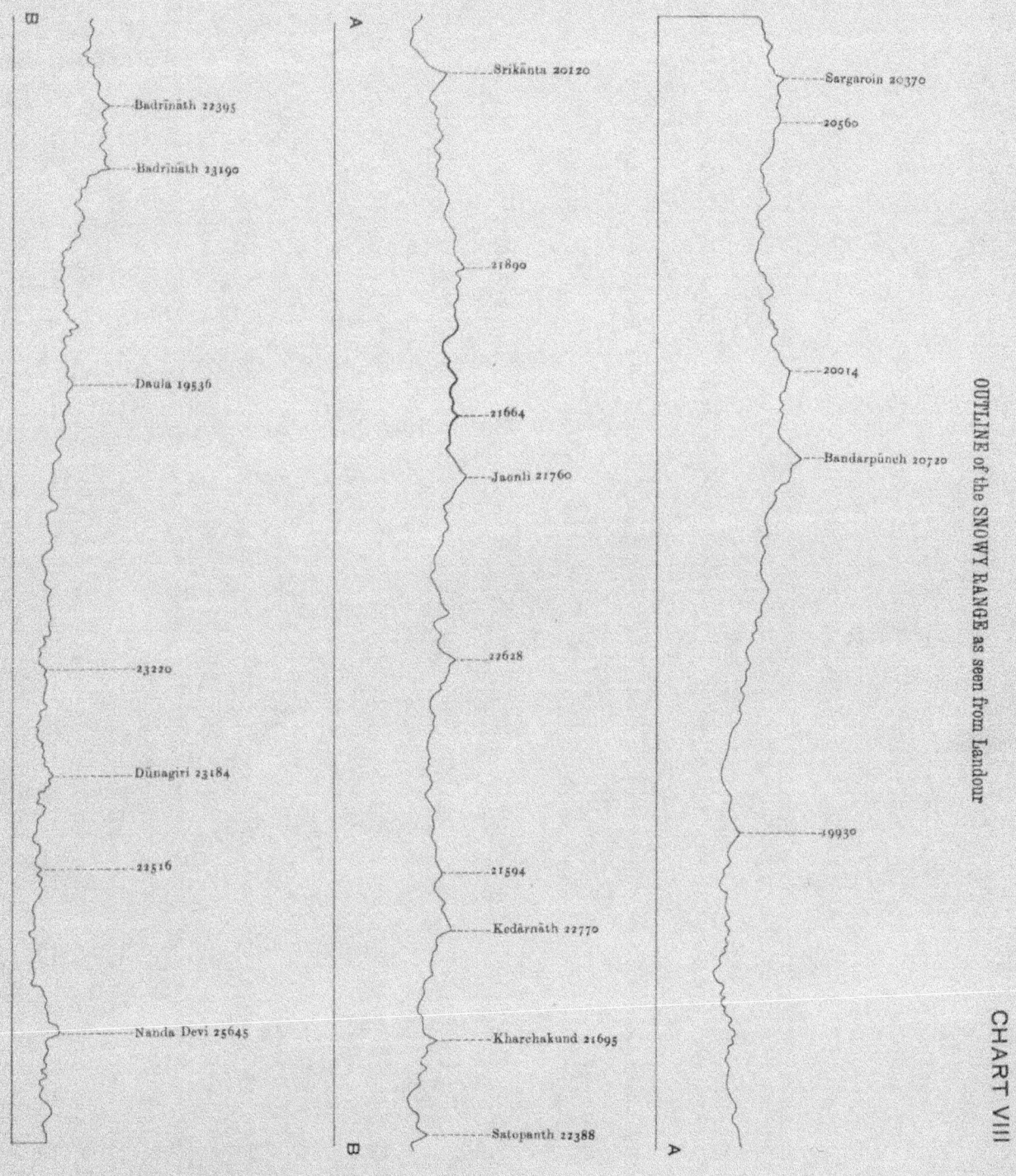

www.ingramcontent.com/pod-product-compliance
Lightning Source LLC
LaVergne TN
LVHW061220060426
835508LV00014B/1377